FORENSICS
FOR KIDS

The Science and History of Crime Solving
With 21 Activities

MELISSA ROSS

**CHICAGO
REVIEW
PRESS**

First edition
Published by Chicago Review Press Incorporated
814 North Franklin Street
Chicago, Illinois 60610
ISBN 978-1-64160-691-2

Library of Congress Control Number: 2021951476

Cover and interior design: Sarah Olson
Cover images: (*front cover*) Magnifying glass over fingerprint, sveta/
stock.adobe.com; Test tubes, Pixel-Shot/stock.adobe.com; Facial
reconstruction model, FBI; Antique pharmacy bottle, Gareth
Howlett/shutterstock.com; Scientist using a microscope, AnnaStills/
shutterstock.com; Car tire print, Couperfield/stock.adobe.com;
Frances Glessner Lee, Glessner House; Forensic expert dusing for
fingerprints, Microgen/stock.adobe.com; (*back cover*) Biometric iris
recognition circle, pngtree.com; Crime scene markers, fusssergei/
stock.adobe.com; Vintage microscope, Zsolt Horvath/stock.adobe
.com; Evidence bag, Shawn Hempel/stock.adobe.com
Interior illustrations: Jim Spence

Printed in the United States of America
5 4 3 2 1

To all those
who love
searching
for the truth
and solving
mysteries.

CONTENTS

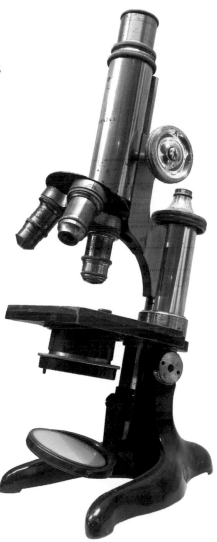

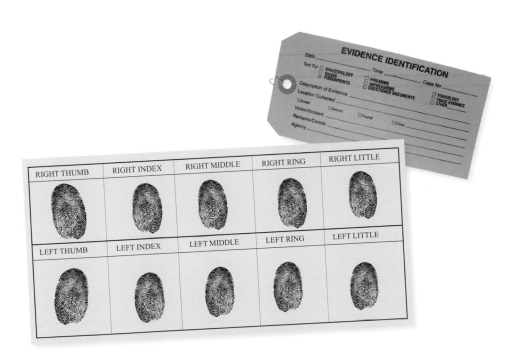

ACKNOWLEDGMENTS

I wish to extend a heartfelt thank-you to "secret, undercover" agent MaryAnn Kohl. You believed in this project before anyone else and remained the enthusiastic cheerleader throughout every step. This wouldn't have happened without you. To each person on the Chicago Review team who worked on this project—thank you for your patience and expertise.

I'm grateful to Jan Peck and all the brilliant writers at the Nest Critique Group. You thoughtfully listened to many excerpts from the manuscript and gave me valuable input and encouragement.

I sincerely appreciate those who graciously took time to share their professional experiences and knowledge with me in interviews: Barrie Schwortz, J. Warner Wallace, Tony Fullman, and Dixie Peters. Thank you for answering my many questions!

To my husband, Robb, and the rest of my family—your love and encouragement kept the wind in my sails on a very long but fascinating forensics journey.

TIME LINE

44 BC First recorded autopsy (Julius Caesar)

1247 First forensic textbook (*Washing Away of Wrongs*) published

1752 First recorded toxicology conviction (Mary Blandy)

1775 Carl Wilhelm Scheele develops arsenic test

1776 Identification of Joseph Warren's body from dentures

1806 Valentine Ross develops more precise arsenic test

1813 Matthew Orfila publishes *Treatise on Poisons*

1829 Metropolitan Police replaces Bow Street Runners

1836 James Marsh develops the Marsh test, a system for detecting arsenic

1840 Marie Lafarge convicted using the Marsh test

1842 Metropolitan Police detective branch forms

1853 Teichmann test for hemoglobin created

1856 Sir William Herschel uses thumbprints on documents

1863 Ballistics solves Gen. Stonewall Jackson's death

1869 Friedrich Miescher discovers DNA

1870 Bertillon system created

1880 Henry Faulds uses fingerprints to solve a crime

1887 First Sherlock Homes novel (*A Study in Scarlet*) published

1888 Bertillon develops mug shots

1891 Hans Gross publishes *Criminal Investigation: A Practical Textbook for Magistrates, Police Officers, and Lawyers*

1892 Sir Francis Galton publishes *Fingerprints*

1893 Mark Twain uses fingerprints in *Pudd'nhead Wilson*

Sir Edward Henry develops Henry Classification System

1901 Karl Landsteiner discovers human blood groups

Paul Uhlenuth invents the precipitin blood test

1902 Henry's fingerprint system leads to conviction

1908 FBI established

1910 Edmond Locard establishes first crime laboratory

1920 Locard's Exchange Principle established

1925 Comparison microscope invented

1927 DeAutrmont brothers apprehended with help of forensics

1929 St. Valentine's Day Massacre solved using forensics

1932 FBI Lab created

Handwriting analysis helps convict Lindbergh kidnapper

1951 Central Identification Lab uses anthropology for identification

1953 Watson, Crick, and Wilkins identify DNA helix structure

1955 United Airlines Flight 629 crash solved using forensics

1972 Bomb-sniffing dog finds bomb on TWA Flight 7

1977 Automated Fingerprint Identification System begins

1981 William Bass establishes the Body Farm

1984 Alec Jeffreys develops DNA profiling test

1988 First conviction using DNA

Morris worm infects computers

US Fish and Wildlife Service Forensics Laboratory is built

1990 Combined DNA Index System (CODIS) database established

1996 Mitochondrial DNA first admitted in court

1999 Integrated Automated Fingerprint Identification System (IAFIS) database

2000 Love Bug infects computer

Biometric identification algorithms develop

2002 ATF Fire Research Lab established

2003 FBI creates Terrorist Explosive Device Analytical Center

2008 Iris recognition used in prisons

2011 Next Generation Identification (NGI) biometric database established

2014 Mobile face recognition adopted by law enforcement agencies

2017 Rapid DNA Act signed

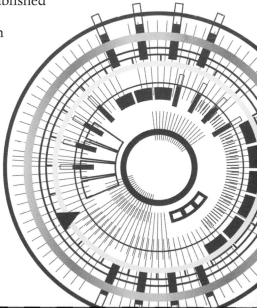

1 WHAT IS FORENSIC SCIENCE?

Suppose you are the investigator of a train robbery. The thieves used dynamite to blow open one of the train cars, hoping to steal the valuables inside. But the criminals accidentally used too much dynamite and destroyed all the loot. Even though their robbery was unsuccessful, they killed innocent men working on the train, making sure to leave no witnesses. The criminals are guilty of homicide and are wanted by every state in the nation for the senseless murders.

Police have gathered a few clues from the scene: a gun, some gun shells, a pair of overalls, and two shoe coverings made out of burlap sacks. They have concluded that there were three men responsible for the crime, but they have no clues as to who the men are. Now, they have contacted you for help. What is the first step you will take to try to discover the three men's identities? What might you learn from the items that were found, and what tools will you use to study them?

THE REAL STORY

This train robbery actually occurred in 1923. The Southern Pacific train was held up in Oregon as it headed toward San Francisco. Police decided to send the items they found at the scene to a chemistry professor named Edward Heinrich at the University of California, Berkeley. Heinrich used scientific methods to study the evidence, something rarely done in crime investigations at the time.

Using a microscope, Heinrich learned that a stain on the overalls was tree sap, and that the dust inside a pocket was from trees. He also found wood chips in another pocket. These discoveries led him to believe that the owner of the overalls was a lumberjack. The overalls' size and shoe covering size helped Heinrich conclude the lumberjack's height and weight. He believed the man was no taller than five foot ten and weighed about 165 pounds.

A wanted poster for the DeAutremont brothers.
National Postal Museum, Smithsonian Institution

Heinrich determined that the lumberjack was about 20 to 25 years old, and after examining tiny strands of hair stuck in one of the buttons of the overalls, he found that the lumberjack had light brown hair. He also used chemicals and magnification to find a hidden serial number on the pistol. He traced the serial number to the person who had purchased the gun, a man named Ray DeAutremont. Ray fit the description of the lumberjack Heinrich was looking for. Yet it still took four years to track Ray and his two brothers down and bring them to justice. Without Heinrich's scientific analysis, they may never have been captured.

THE SCIENCE OF SOLVING CRIMES

Resolving the Southern Pacific train mystery required science. Collecting and testing evidence found at a crime scene is called *forensic science*. Back in 1923, when the DeAutremont brothers held up the train, there were no forensic labs in the United States in which to study evidence. Forensic labs existed only in Europe. Professor Heinrich had to conduct his experiments in his home.

Today there are numerous forensic labs all over the country dedicated to studying evidence from crime scenes. Many types of science are used in these labs such as biology, physics, chemistry, and anthropology, to name a few. In forensics, the information gained by studying crime scene evidence is then shared in a court of law. In short, forensics is the use of scientific methods to solve crimes.

CHINESE FORENSICS

In the ancient Western world, there was not much science available to help with solving crimes. Back then, crime solving was mainly based on testimonies from victims and witnesses. But there were no scientific methods to distinguish truths from lies. The testimony of those the ruling authorities liked would hold more weight than the testimony of anyone the authorities did not like. This type of crime solving resulted in many innocent people being convicted of crimes they did not commit. Others who were actually guilty often got away with their crimes, never being held accountable.

However, at the time, the Chinese were a bit more scientific. In 1247, the first forensic textbook was published, titled *The Washing Away of Wrongs*. The author, Song Ci (Sung Tz'u), was a medical expert, and today is considered the father of forensic science in China. When his book was written, bureaucrats working under the king in China oversaw investigations of suspicious deaths. This included examinations of corpses. The problem was that these officials had no training for this type of job. Song Ci wrote *The Washing Away of Wrongs* as a guidebook to help them in conducting investigations.

Song Ci's book covered subjects such as the difference between males' and females' bone structure, and determining the time of death from examining a corpse. While we now know that much of the information he provided was inaccurate, it is interesting to see that the Chinese saw the need for using science in crime scene

Mystery Robbery

Imagine you are a detective in Britain during the year 1775 and have been asked to lead the investigation of a robbery. Below is an image of the scene of the crime. On a piece of paper, write a short summary of what you see in your own words. Your summary is the official documentation of the crime. Then answer the questions the local authorities are asking you.

To make things more difficult, during this time period in Europe, there was no fingerprint system, no criminal mug shots to refer to, no photography or video, and no blood tests. Investigators were very limited in how to record, collect, and test evidence.

The scene description (see illustration) taken by the police: A local pharmacy was broken into sometime in the middle of the night. A window was shattered, possibly for entry. The cash box was taken. It contained sales earnings from two full days, according to the pharmacist.

When questioned about the location of the box, he confided that he had become lazy about hiding it well or locking it up. The medicine shelf had been knocked to the floor. Medicine of all kinds—powders and liquids—was found all over the floor. A few of the bottles were broken, but not all. Two broken bottles were next to an opposite wall. The pharmacist says he cannot tell what medicine, if any, is gone because of the mixed-up mess. There were no witnesses.

Now it's your turn to investigate. Write your observations of the scene, exactly what you see. Make sure to describe the scene as accurately as possible because your written record is the only reference you will have.

Once you have written your description, see if you can answer the following questions the authorities may ask you:

How did it look like the robber broke in?

- What tool/tools might have been used?

- How do you think the bottles by the wall were broken?

- Is there any evidence left that might be directly linked to the criminal?

- Could some of the medicines have been removed?

- What, if any, are the next steps you will take to discover a suspect?

- Is there any evidence from the scene you should collect and test? If so, how will you go about doing this?

- Have you developed a hypothesis from your observations? What do you think might be some of the motives for such a crime?

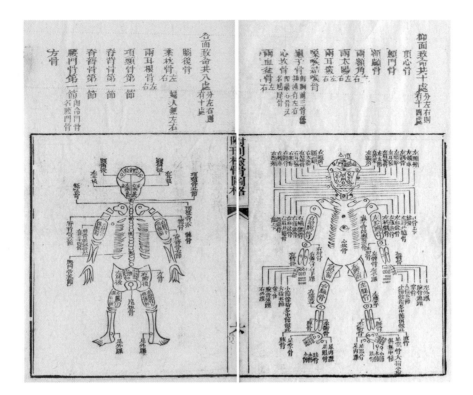

investigations. They attempted to use forensic methods using the limited science available to them at the time.

One case example Song Ci (Tz'u Sung) notes in his book involves a man who was murdered in a small Chinese village. The murder weapon was a sickle, a sharp tool used for harvesting rice. To find the person responsible, the investigators ordered all the suspects to come together in one outside area. They were told to place their sickles on the ground in front of them in the hot sun. Everyone stood quietly wondering what the investigators were waiting for.

After a while, flies began to gather on only one of the sickles, the one used by the criminal. The flies were attracted to the blood and tissue left on the blade, remains that were too small for people to see. The culprit had been found, and the owner

Entomology

Forensic entomology is the study of insects related to criminal investigation. When a human body is found, investigators need to understand how the person died and how long ago he or she died. A forensic entomologist can help answer these questions.

When a corpse decomposes, it goes through many stages of decay. Each stage of decomposition attracts different types of insects such as flies, mites, and beetles. Entomologists know which type of insect appears at each stage.

The most commonly studied insect in forensic entomology is flies. Flies lay eggs, and maggots hatch from them. Entomologists understand the time frame of a maggot's development. They know how it relates to the decomposition of a body. By examining the insects, they can tell not only how long ago the person died, but many other details, such as if the body was moved.

Many factors can affect the decomposition of a corpse, such as the weather and the area where the body has been discovered. It is important that forensic entomologists have learned how decomposition is affected by each of these different factors.

of the sickle realized he was caught and confessed. It is the first documented case of entomology used to solve a crime. Entomology is the scientific study of insects.

Although the procedures Song Ci wrote about were very naive compared to the scientific methods available today, the Chinese did see the necessity for science in criminal investigations well before others thought about it at all. It took the Western world much longer to do the same. In Europe, forensics evolved slowly over time as new scientific and medical discoveries were made.

FORENSICS BEGINS IN THE WESTERN WORLD

Years ago, Europe had no system for examining bodies to determine how someone died. Officials called *coroners* looked into suspicious deaths, along with performing their other duties, but like the bureaucrats in China, coroners were not physicians. Their investigations were simply observations rather than scientific studies. But because of their importance, death investigations pushed forensics forward. As Song Ci put it, "There is nothing more important than human life."

As medicine advanced, forensic science followed along behind it. In 1347, a very important event impacted the medical community profoundly: merchant ships arrived in Italy bringing a deadly illness called the *bubonic plague*. Most of the sailors on the ships were already deceased, and the ones remaining were very sick. This horrible

The Autopsy of Julius Caesar

One of the first recorded autopsies was that of the famous Roman dictator Julius Caesar. Caesar was assassinated on March 15, 1944 BC by members of his own Senate. The team of 23 men surrounded him and stabbed him 23 times. In this way, no one man was responsible for his murder.

A physician named Antistius performed an autopsy, which a Roman historian of the time described in a detailed report. The conclusion that Antistius came to after his examination was that only one of the stab wounds actually killed Caesar, the one that punctured his aorta, near his heart. All the other wounds were not substantial enough to have caused his death.

In 2003, a group of modern forensic scientists decided to reinvestigate Julius Caesar's murder using new technology. This time, the autopsy was conducted with digital software. Following the ancient autopsy report, they created a 3D image of Caesar's body with stab wounds. They studied the attack on Caesar. The investigators found that it would have been impossible for all 23 men to have actually stabbed Caesar. They theorized that only 5 to 10 men could have actually struck him.

The Murder of Caesar **by Karl von Piloty.** *Wikimedia Commons*

disease spread across Europe for the next five years, killing more than 20 million people. Known as the Black Death, the disease struck quickly, and even infected animals. Europe was devastated by loss and fear. No one understood how the disease spread or what to do to stop it.

We know now that the bubonic plague was caused by a bacterium called *Yersinia pestis*, but back in the 14th century it was a complete mystery. Physicians used a method called *bloodletting* to try to help patients infected with the disease. Bloodletting was a common practice used by doctors during that time to help those who were sick. Doctors believed that an ill person could be cured by draining infected blood from his or her body.

After the plague subsided, people were very interested in learning about illnesses and what to do about them. Autopsies (dissections of human corpses) were performed in order to understand diseases and their progression in the human body. William Harvey, an English doctor, learned new information from autopsies about blood and the way it circulates in the body. He discovered that bloodletting was not something that helped people but could actually kill them. This was just one of the new medical advances that came about from autopsies.

Criminal investigators saw how much valuable information the medical community was learning. They realized that autopsies could help them in their work as well. By the end of the 16th century, autopsies became part of many criminal death investigations. Yet even then, one had to know how to find the right information, the information that would tell examiners if the death was a homicide or not.

POISON PROBLEMS

For centuries, poisons posed a real problem for those investigating suspicious deaths. Poisons were a favorite murder weapon because they were so difficult to detect. Many poisons made the death appear as though the victim had died naturally because they created symptoms like common diseases of the day.

Arsenic was an especially popular poison. Transparent and odorless, arsenic could easily be hidden in food without anyone noticing. It was also a fairly common household item, often purchased for purposes such as killing rats. A greedy

An 1889 advertisement for Arsenic Complexion Wafers.
Wikimedia Commons

A Woman's Face Is Her Fortune.

DR. SIMM'S ARSENIC COMPLEXION WAFERS

After a few days' use will permanently remove all Blotches, Moles, Pimples and Freckles, producing an Entrancingly Beautiful Complexion that shames the use of powders and creams. Warranted perfectly harmless.   Sold by all leading druggists at $1 per box of 100 wafers.

Dr. Simms' Safe Periodical Wafers are sure and reliable for all female irregularities.   Price $2 per box.   Sent by mail (secure) on receipt of price.   Warranted to contain no "Tansy" for "Pennyroyal."

THUMLER & Co., 83 Chambers St., New York.
H. M. Parchen & Co., Sole Agents, Helena.

Powder Experiment

Five containers of powders were found at a crime scene. You will test each one and record your findings to determine what each one is.

You'll Need

- volunteer
- ½ cup cornstarch
- ½ cup baking soda
- ½ cup baby powder
- ½ cup salt
- ½ cup sugar
- ¼ cup water
- ¼ cup vinegar
- iodine
- dropper
- paper plate
- plastic spoons
- 7 jars or plastic cups

1. Have a friend place the cornstarch, baking soda, baking powder, salt, and sugar in separate jars or cups and label them A, B, C, D, and E. They must be sure to record the type of substance represented by each letter on a piece of paper.

2. Now you will test the powders in order to determine what each one is. First, record a description of each powder.

3. Drop a spoonful of each powder into a small jar of clean water, stir, then record the results for each one. Did it dissolve, become murky, etc.?

4. Drop a spoonful of each powder into a small jar of clean vinegar. Record the reaction of each powder.

5. Place a spoonful of each powder on a paper plate and put a few drops of iodine on each powder. Record the results.

6. Compare your findings from the "unknown" powders to the "known" powders. Based on your findings, what do you think each "unknown" powder is?

and heartless relative wanting his or her inheritance early might see arsenic as a solution. By the 17th century, arsenic poisoning had become so widespread in France it was called *poudre de succession*, which means "inheritance powder."

Forensic science came up with methods to help solve these unsolvable poison cases. The first such case occurred in 1752. Mary Blandy lived with her father, who had given his consent to her marriage to Capt. William Henry Cranstoun. But when he found out that Cranstoun was actually still married to another woman, he would not allow Cranstoun to see his daughter. Soon, Mary's father became ill each time he ate. Mary confessed to her father before he died that she had placed a white powder in his meals. She told him that Cranstoun had given her a special mood powder to place in her father's food, and that Cranstoun had assured her it would cause her father to feel better about him. Mary claimed she had not realized the powder was poison, even though his sickness increased after each meal.

Although there were no standard scientific tests for arsenic poisoning at the time, Dr. Anthony Addington, the medical examiner, suspected arsenic poisoning. His suspicions led him to heat the white powder he found on a piece of hot iron. After hitting the heat, the powder gave off a garlic-scented cloud. Addington knew that this reaction was exactly what happens when arsenic is heated. This, and a few other tests he performed, convinced the jury that Mary had poisoned her father. The jury found Mary Blandy guilty of murder and sentenced her to death by hanging.

The Blandy case was the first documented investigation where the science of toxicology (detecting poisons and their effects) was used in an arsenic poisoning conviction. The tests Addison employed were simple, though, and later could easily be refuted by cunning lawyers.

TACKLING THE PROBLEM WITH SCIENCE

The common practice of poisoning inspired chemists to develop methods that could uncover the existence of arsenic in the human body. This was not an easy job. It required a lot of testing and studying.

In 1775, a Swedish chemist named Carl Wilhelm Scheele created a test that could detect arsenic in human bodies, but only in large amounts. Often victims were poisoned with small amounts over time, which his test could not uncover. But in 1806 Valentin Ross, a German chemist, developed a more precise test that could find arsenic in the stomach walls of a victim.

Then Mathieu Orfila, a medical chemistry professor in Paris, improved the testing further. In 1813 he wrote a book titled *Treatise on Poisons*, a guidebook for those investigating the use of poisons. Orfila was determined to help make

James Marsh.
Wikimedia Commons

chemical analysis of poisons a recognized part of forensic medicine. His book was an important advancement. Orfila became known as an expert in toxicology and was even asked to testify in many court cases.

Arsenic test results were still not always as accurate as they needed to be to hold up in court. A chemist in Britain named James Marsh was called on to perform an arsenic test on evidence in a trial in 1832. A young man was suspected of killing his grandfather by poisoning his coffee with arsenic. Marsh was convinced the grandson was guilty, but the arsenic test he used showed otherwise.

Marsh saw that the inaccuracy of the arsenic test resulted in a murderer getting away with his crime. He was so angry that he became determined to create a more accurate test, and he succeeded. His new test was called the Marsh test. It was so exact that even a tiny amount of arsenic could be found in a human corpse. It took a while for people to become aware of the Marsh test and to trust its accuracy, though.

THE SPOTLIGHT SHINES ON FORENSIC SCIENCE

In 1840, the Marsh test was used in the widely publicized Lafarge murder case. Twenty-four-year-old Marie Lafarge was on trial for the murder of her husband, Charles. Marie claimed that the arsenic witnesses saw her purchase was meant to kill the rats in her house. She denied poisoning her husband.

Forensic Toxicology

Forensic toxicologists can determine if drugs were used in a crime and if so, what kinds. Samples they test include blood, tissue, powders, liquids, urine, saliva, and even hair. They can determine if an illegal drug such as heroin is present in the sample, or perhaps a legal drug prescribed for an illness.

Toxicologists perform two types of tests. *Qualitative tests* determine what a substance is. *Quantitative tests* determine the amount of a substance. Many chemicals are harmless at certain doses but become a deadly potion when consumed in larger amounts.

Toxicologists use qualitative tests to separate the components that make up a particular substance. With these methods of separation, the toxicologist can find out exactly what a particular substance is made of.

Doctors performed chemical tests on Charles's body, but Marie's lawyers constantly questioned the doctor's abilities and findings. The doctors were unaware of the Marsh test, so it was not hard to shed doubt on the other arsenic tests they were using. It seemed there was no way to determine for sure if Marie had actually poisoned Charles.

Hoping to find conclusive evidence, the judge ordered Charles Lafarge's body to be exhumed for more tests. Journalists filled newspapers with the growing story and increasing drama. Everyone was reading about the Lafarge trial.

Finally, Mathieu Orfila, the top expert in toxicology, was called on, creating even more curiosity. Orfila performed the Marsh test on samples from

Crime Scene Dollhouses

Dollhouses were not something to play around with for Frances Glessner Lee. They were serious training tools for forensic investigators. Lee learned how to create miniature settings when she was growing up. Much later in life, she realized how these intricate creations could help investigators learn to observe small pieces of important evidence.

Lee became interested in crime from a friend named George Magrath, who was a medical examiner. She also read about crimes in newspapers and even visited real crime scenes. She saw how investigators often missed important details and realized they needed better training. A wealthy woman, Lee helped start the Department of Legal Medicine at Harvard Medical School in the 1930s. There, criminal investigators and law enforcement officials attended forensic seminars.

Lee decided to create dollhouses to help with their training. With assistance from a carpenter, she created 20 miniature houses or apartments. Each scene was based on a mixture of real and imagined homicides.

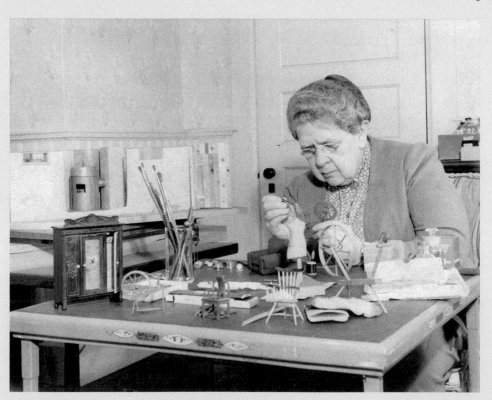

Frances Glessner Lee building one of her "Nutshell Studies of Unexplained Death." *Glessner House*

The carpenter fashioned the furniture, floors, and windows. Lee sewed and knitted each piece of clothing, upholstery, and linen. Detailed paintings and tiny household items completed each room. She even created the covers of miniscule books and newspapers. Lee encouraged those studying the dollhouse crime scenes to search systematically for important evidence and clues.

Her collection of scenes is called the Nutshell Studies of Unexplained Death and are still used in training students today. Frances Glessner Lee is often referred to as the mother of forensic science, one of the few women in her day working in the field of forensics.

Charles Lafarge's body. Orfila also tested samples from the grave soil surrounding Lafarge's, body because soil sometimes contains natural traces of arsenic. He proved with the Marsh test that there were definite traces of arsenic in Lafarge's body, and that it did not come from the soil he was buried in.

Marie Lafarge was found guilty of murder. The deadly season of rampant poisoning in Europe was finally slowing down. Forensic science was now beginning to bloom where everyone could see it.

SKULLS AND SKELETONS IN THE CLASSROOM

Forensics was still not considered a recognized science in the early 1800s, however. That would require education and more advances in medicine. Medical colleges in Great Britain started offering lectures on investigations of deaths. In 1844, France even created a department of forensic medicine at a university in the city of Lyon. A physician named Alexandre Lacassagne was chosen to lead it.

Lacassagne believed a professor should do more than just give lectures. He often allowed students to take part in the real criminal investigations he himself was working on. Lacassagne's students helped him perform many criminal autopsies in his large amphitheater classroom. Students were given observation charts to help them follow step-by-step procedures as they investigated the cause of death.

Lacassagne also had a museum containing many artifacts from real crimes such as guns, bullets, knives, and swords. There were skulls and skeletons, hair and poisons. Many of Lacassage's students became well-known forensic professionals in the new forensic field.

Alexandre Lacassagne.
Wikimedia Commons

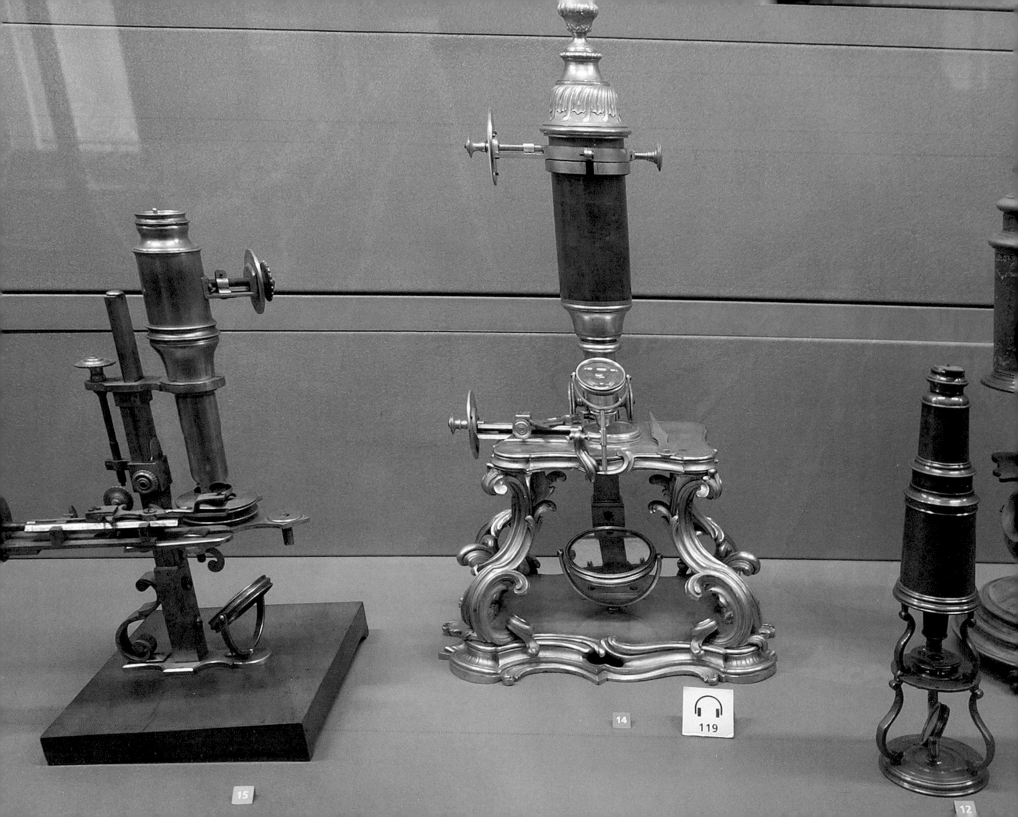

15

14

119

12

FORENSIC SCIENCE IN THE 19TH CENTURY

2

A classroom of quiet students can suddenly turn into chaos without the presence of a teacher. Maybe you have experienced this firsthand when a teacher has stepped out of your classroom. But as soon as the teacher returns, so does the quiet. The presence of authority can keep behavior in check. For centuries the approach to handling crime was much like this—keep it from happening in the first place.

In Great Britain during the 18th century, watchmen were assigned to patrol the streets from 9 o'clock at night until sunrise. They also lit streetlamps to keep criminals from lurking in the dark. Eventually, daytime patrols were added.

Much responsibility also rested on citizens. A person who witnessed someone breaking the law was expected to follow the criminal and yell for help. Those who turned in offenders were rewarded with money. As city populations grew, so did the crime and the need for change.

STOP THE CRIME

London grew into a crowded city during the 1700s. To help with crime there, Henry and John Fielding organized the Bow Street Runners in 1749. Starting with just six men, the Bow Street Runners were hired to apprehend criminals and to patrol certain areas, either on horseback or on foot. The headquarters on Bow Street became a place where people could bring information about specific crimes. This helped solve some crimes, but a more effective force was needed to really make a difference in deterring crime.

In 1829, the Metropolitan Police Act established by Sir Robert Peel replaced the watchmen and Bow Street patrols. Three thousand men were hired to be a part of the new Metropolitan Police. These uniformed officers were called *bobbies*, and they carried wooden batons, handcuffs, and eventually a whistle. They patrolled the streets in order to keep criminal activity down.

The creation of this police force definitely reduced the amount of minor offenses, but it wasn't enough to fight the mounting crime. In 1842, a detective agency was created within the

---

Scotland Yard

In the early 19th century, the city of London was growing rapidly. The Metropolitan Police began as the new law enforcement to handle the increasing crime. The first police headquarters had an entrance that opened onto a large courtyard called Great Scotland Yard. At one time, the courtyard site contained a medieval palace where Scottish royalty stayed when visiting London. Over time, Scotland Yard became synonymous with the Metropolitan Police.

When the Metropolitan Police force first began, it was not exactly trusted. In 1842, Scotland Yard assigned a small number of plainclothes police officers to oversee certain areas in London. The public thought of them as spies. Eventually, when citizens saw the positive results of Scotland Yard's crime control, they changed their minds. From that small group of officers, Scotland Yard has now grown into a department of more than 30,000 officers.

Within Scotland Yard is a department called the Criminal Investigation Department (CID), which oversees investigations of crimes. Its many divisions include a police lab, fingerprint experts, detective training, and a special force called the Flying Squad.

Today the Metropolitan Police is in a new, larger location on the River Thames at Victoria Embankment. The new headquarters is called the New Scotland Yard.

Sign outside the New Scotland Yard.
Wikimedia Commons

Metropolitan Police. These men would not only discourage crimes but also investigate them.

PINKERTON'S NATIONAL DETECTIVE AGENCY

While Scotland Yard was the main crime-fighting agency in London, the Pinkerton agency filled that role in the United States. The founder, Allan Pinkerton, did not start out planning to be a detective. He immigrated from Scotland in 1819 and opened a shop near Chicago that specialized in barrel making. He was a strong abolitionist, and his shop is said to have been a stopping place for runaway slaves on their way to freedom.

One day, Pinkerton came across a gang of counterfeiters, and with his help, authorities were able to arrest the men. After that, he was hired as a deputy sheriff. Eventually, in 1850 he decided to open up his own detective agency.

Pinkerton's National Detective Agency worked across state lines with law enforcement. They also provided private security services for several railway companies. In addition, his agency was hired to collect information for the Union army during the Civil War.

The Pinkerton agency used wanted posters to help apprehend criminals. Each poster included a photo, name, physical description, and reward. It was also the first agency in the United States to create a system of mug shots called a rogues' gallery. It included photos of wanted men with detailed information about them.

In 1861, Pinkerton became the first agency in the United States to hire a woman detective. Her name was Kate Warne. She was 23 years old and convinced Pinkerton that the agency needed a woman detective. She could disguise herself and go undercover where men could not.

One of the most famous cases Warne was part of involved President Abraham Lincoln. Pinkerton became aware of a plan to assassinate Lincoln

Left to right: **Allan Pinkerton, President Abraham Lincoln, and Maj. Gen. John A. McClernand, 1862.** *Library of Congress (LC-B817-7949)*

in Baltimore on his way to the Capitol. After Pinkerton informed Lincoln, the president was secretly smuggled through the area at night. Lincoln posed as Kate Warne's invalid brother as they boarded a train, and no one knew he was on the train while Warne guarded him the entire trip.

The Pinkerton National Detective Agency still exists today, known simply as Pinkerton.

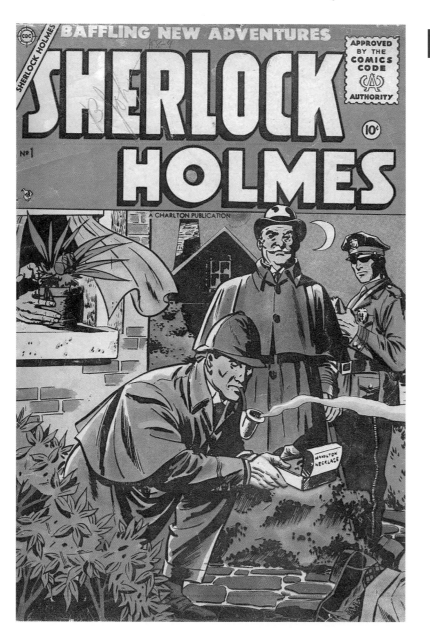

SHERLOCK HOLMES LEADS THE WAY

The time was ripe for an extraordinary detective to emerge. He would be a genius who would know how to use logic, keen observation, and science to solve crimes. His name was Sherlock Holmes, and he emerged for the first time in 1887. He was only a fictional character from a series of novels, but his effect on the development of forensic investigation was very real.

The author of the Sherlock Holmes stories was a medical doctor named Arthur Conan Doyle. He based the character of Sherlock Holmes on a professor he had studied under named Joseph Bell. Professor Bell had an incredible knack for observing small details. He could determine where a person had been and his occupation, just by noticing how he walked and the soot on his shoes. He taught his students, like Doyle, to be keen observers as well.

In Doyle's stories, Holmes was not only a genius observer—in the area of forensics he was ahead of his time. In the first novel, *A Study in Scarlet*, Holmes even had a lab in which to conduct experiments on evidence from crime scenes. At the time there was no such lab in the real world of criminal investigation.

Over the years, Holmes used a variety of forensic methods. In the story "A Case of Identity," written in 1891, Holmes practiced a new forensic technique. He was able to examine the unique marks of a specific typewriter to identify a suspect. Holmes was also an expert in footprint analysis and handwriting analysis. He developed a test that could even determine if a substance was blood before there really was such a test.

A few of the many other areas of expertise Holmes used to solve crimes included trace analysis, decoding ciphers, and the use of dogs to help solve crimes. He could observe a person's gait (walking stride) to determine identity as well. (Of course, it was much easier to create successful forensic science in fiction than in the real world. That took time—time for scientists to experiment and learn. Still, Holmes inspired them to press forward to help make forensic fiction become reality.)

The public was enthralled, including people entering the new forensic field. Holmes became their inspiration. This was true of a man named Edmond Locard, who became known as the Sherlock Holmes of France.

EDMOND LOCARD: "EVERY CONTACT LEAVES A TRACE"

After graduating from medical school in 1902, Edmond Locard served as a classroom assistant to the famous Alexandre Lacassagne. He also worked as a medical examiner during World War I. Locard was so interested in applying science to law that he earned a law degree on top of his PhD in medicine. He also wrote a seven-volume series titled *Traité de criminalistique (Forensic Treatise)*. In that book, he described what came to be known as Locard's Exchange Principle, the principle on which modern forensics is based.

Locard's famous exchange principle states that "every contact leaves a trace." This simply means that people at a crime scene will leave traces of themselves behind and take traces of the scene with them when they leave. When you sit on a couch watching television, you are leaving small pieces of yourself behind. Your fingerprints are on the remote control, and hair from your head or arms may have fallen on the floor. Maybe a thread from your clothes was left, or a footprint from your shoe. You also took parts of the room with you when you left. A small fiber off the couch may have attached to your jeans, or cat hair to your shoe. These traces are pieces of evidence that can be found and analyzed. With that one principle, Locard changed the field of forensics forever.

Passionate about forensics, Locard traveled to many different police departments, even in the United States. He wanted to learn more about their methods of crime solving and sought to learn ways to improve investigations. He decided that investigators needed a lab to study evidence collected from crime scenes, similar to the one Sherlock Holmes had. He could not convince others of the need for such a thing, so in 1910 he set up the first forensics lab in a few attic rooms. He purchased his own supplies, including a microscope and chemicals. In time, he proved

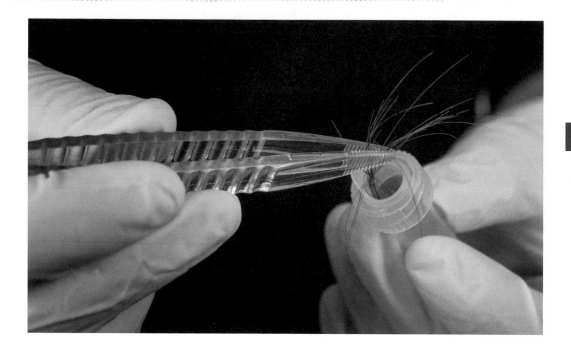

Collecting hair samples.
iStock/SandraMatic

that his methods were quite successful at solving crimes.

The cases Locard solved were ones brought to him because other investigators could not figure them out. One such case involved the use of counterfeit coins for purchases. When police finally apprehended three suspects, they could not collect enough evidence to prove that the men were responsible for using the fake money.

Locard asked for the suspects' clothing to be sent to his lab so he could study it. Using a magnifying glass and a pair of tweezers, he carefully removed dust from certain areas on the clothes. Applying chemicals to test the dust particles, he learned that there were tiny amounts of tin, antimony, and lead that matched the exact makeup of the counterfeit coins. With this clear evidence

against them, the three men confessed to the police. As Locard helped solve more and more cases, people began to see how important a lab was in helping to solve crimes.

LEARNING TO SECURE AND RECORD CRIME SCENES

In the 1800s, there were few real forensic examination methods available to study the evidence found at crime scenes. At most crime scenes, investigators would walk around freely looking for clues. They were not as concerned about harming evidence back then because there were not many tests available to study what they found.

Austrian investigator Hans Gross understood how important handling a crime scene is to an investigation, long before others of his day. In 1893, he wrote a book titled *Criminal Investigation: A Practical Textbook for Magistrates, Police Officers, and Lawyers*. In his book, he stressed the importance of not handling evidence until it is thoroughly documented. As obvious as this seems to us today, this was a new kind of thinking in the 1800s. His book made a huge impact on the investigation world. Slowly, investigators began securing crime scenes more effectively.

Another change was taking place at this time: an invention called photography, which gave people a new way to record events. Yet even after its invention, it took a while for investigators to learn how to use photographs in criminal investigations.

It is hard for us to imagine what life was like before photography. Today it is at everyone's fingertips. We keep a record on our phone without even realizing it. With our cameras, we record our friends, places we have gone, and family events. But imagine if you left a room and later tried to remember every detail you saw there without having taken any pictures. Prior to the invention of photography, recording a crime scene could be done only by taking handwritten notes and by remembering what it looked like.

ALPHONSE BERTILLON, CRIME SCENE PHOTOGRAPHY, AND THE BERTILLON SYSTEM

Alphonse Bertillon became a leader in forensics in the 1800s even though he started out as just a clerk in a Paris police station. He grew up in a scientific family and recognized the need for science in crime solving. He saw how sloppily photos were taken at crime scenes, if they were even taken at all.

He decided to create a standard method of taking these photos. Pictures of the scene were taken from two different angles. One was a "bird's-eye view," shot from above, and the second was a straight-on view, more at eye level. He also used grids to show the size and dimensions of objects at the crime scene. Bertillon realized photos could also help keep track of criminals if they were taken correctly and organized. He developed a system where a front and profile view of each

Hair Analysis

Trace evidence is very small, sometimes just a few strands of hair. In this activity, you will examine "found" hair strands to see if you can find a match with the "known" ones.

You'll Need

- 2 pulled hair strands from each of six willing people
- 2 pulled hair strands from your own head
- 2 sheets of white paper
- tape
- sandwich baggie marked Unknown
- magnifying glass

1. Place one of the pulled hairs from each head into the Unknown bag. Shake the bag and mix the hairs up.

2. Place the other hair from each head on a sheet of white paper, tape it down, and write the name of the person each hair came from below it.

3. Open the bag of Unknown hairs and place each hair strand on a second sheet of white paper.

4. Using a magnifying glass, try and match the Unknown hair strands to the known ones. Were you able to identify each strand?

Forensic Photography

Before any evidence is collected, a photographer takes pictures of the entire crime scene and all the evidence it contains. Imagine you are the forensic photographer. Record the "crime scene" using photography.

You'll Need

- camera or phone with camera
- paper and pencil or computer

1. Photograph your kitchen before a meal or a family room before company comes over. Take many different photos to record the details of the scene. Take some from above looking down and others straight on. Place a ruler near objects for size reference. Be sure and save your photos in a way that you know these are the BEFORE photos.

2. Now, photograph the scene again after the company has left or the meal has been eaten but not entirely cleaned up. Make sure to use different angles and close-ups as well as the full scene. Compare your BEFORE photos with the AFTER ones. What kind of information have you learned from the photographs as to what exactly happened in the room?

3. On a sheet of paper or computer, record at least 10 observations that indicate what may have happened during the meal or event.

arrested person was taken and placed on index cards. The cards were filed and became the first type of mug shots ever made.

Bertillon became most famous, however, for a new identification system he created called the Bertillon system. Bertillon believed that certain human features remain the same throughout life and that they can be measured with instruments. He also believed that each person's measurements are unique.

With his new system, officers were trained to take measurements of certain features from people in custody. Head circumference, arm length, and left-foot length were a few of the measurements they took. These measurements were then recorded on index cards and filed systematically along with photos of the individual.

But there were several problems with Bertillonnage, as some called it. It was time consuming and expensive to train officers how to measure correctly. Often, two officers came up with different measurements of the same person. But even with all its imperfections, Bertillon's system became the official system of identification everywhere, including the United States. It was the start of a scientific way of looking at criminal identification.

The Bertillon system functioned fairly well until an event in the United States in 1903 at the Leavenworth Prison. When a man named Will West was admitted to the prison, the admitting officer was confused. How could it be possible? Will's measurements matched those of a man named William West already serving time there. Even the photos looked almost exactly the same!

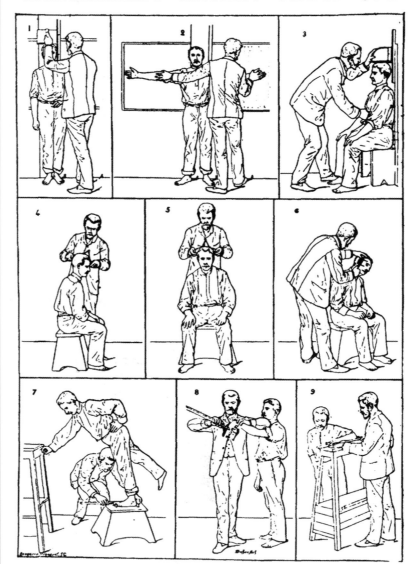

RELEVÉ
DU
SIGNALEMENT ANTHROPOMÉTRIQUE

1. Taille. — 2. Envergure. — 3. Buste. —
4. Longueur de la tête. — 5. Largeur de la tête. — 6. Oreille droite. —
7. Pied gauche. — 8. Médius gauche. — 9. Coudée gauche.

The Bertillon system.
Wikimedia Commons

Anthropometric Measuring

Before the use of fingerprints, the Bertillon system was used for identification. Even with training, two officers using the Bertillon method would often come up with different measurements. See how it works for you and a friend.

You'll Need

- measuring tape
- paper and pencil
- volunteer

1. Number a sheet of paper from 1 to 9 to record the measurements below. These are Bertillon measurements.

2. **Height:** Using a measuring tape, measure the height of your friend as he or she stands against a wall.

3. **Trunk:** Stretch the measuring tape from the ground to the top of the head as your friend sits in a chair. Try to keep the measuring tape as straight as possible.

4. **Reach:** Have your friend stand against a wall and put his or her left arm straight out against the wall parallel with the floor. Measure the tip of the longest left finger to the top of the left shoulder.

5. **Head length:** While your friend sits in a chair, measure from the top of the bridge of the nose to the back of the head where the head meets the neck.

6. **Head width:** Measure from the top of one ear over the top of the head to the other ear.

7. **Ear:** Measure the left ear from the lowest tip straight to the top of the ear.

8. **Left hand:** Measure from the point where the wrist meets the hand to the tip of the longest finger.

9. **Left foot:** While your friend stands only on the left foot, measure from the longest toe to the back of the heel.

10. **Forearm:** While the left arm is bent in a 90-degree angle, measure the arm from the tip of the elbow to the tip of the long finger.

11. Then have someone else measure the same friend's Bertillon measurements.

12. Compare their measurements with yours. Were they the same?

The two men claimed they were not related and did not even know each other, although later it was learned that they were in fact twins. Still, it became clear that it was time for a more reliable identification system, and there was one already brewing.

FINDING FINGERPRINTS

Two men, both from Great Britain, were experimenting with fingerprints about the same time, although they were working in different parts of the world.

The first was Henry Faulds, a physician and missionary working in Japan. He noticed that Japanese potters left fingerprints on their pottery. This ignited his curiosity about fingerprints and led him to collect and study them. He discovered that fingerprints were each unique and realized the importance they could play in solving crimes, especially after he solved one himself.

In 1879 the Japanese police, knowing about Faulds's work with fingerprints, asked for his help with a burglary. Dirty fingerprints had been left on a wall. The police had arrested a suspect, but they had no conclusive evidence if the man was in fact guilty. Faulds collected fingerprints from the man in custody and compared them to those found at the scene. Because they did not match, the man was freed.

Several days later, the police arrested another suspect whose fingerprints *did* match the ones at the crime scene, and the case was solved. When he returned to Great Britain, Faulds excitedly told the Metropolitan Police (Scotland Yard) of his

Fingerprints and Fiction

You may be familiar with Mark Twain's two famous books called *The Adventures of Tom Sawyer* and *The Adventures of Huckleberry Finn*. In 1883, Twain also wrote a series of stories about his life called *Life on the Mississippi*. One of the stories included a character who used a fingerprint as evidence in a crime. Then, in 1893, Twain decided to use fingerprints in his fiction book called *Pudd'nhead Wilson*. In this story, a main character collects fingerprints to actually solve a crime.

The remarkable thing is that fingerprints were not used in the real crime world when these stories were written. It wasn't until 1901 that Scotland Yard began using Sir Edward Henry's fingerprint system to solve crimes. Like Conan Doyle, who created Sherlock Holmes, Mark Twain was a step ahead of the real forensic world.

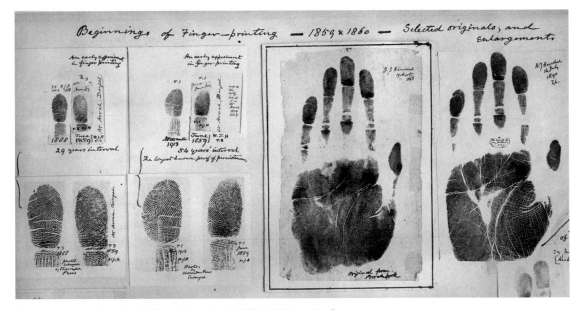

Fingerprints taken by William Herschel, 1859. *Wikimedia Commons*

Fingerprints

Fingerprints are collected in several different ways. Afterward, they are examined and classified into one of three groups. Finally, the individual characteristics are analyzed.

See if you can collect and classify your own fingerprint.

COLLECTING FINGERPRINTS

You'll Need

- ink pad
- white index cards
- olive oil
- baby powder
- old makeup brush
- dirt
- tempera paint
- tape

You can collect your fingerprints in several ways.

1. Press your thumb onto the ink pad, then carefully press it onto a white index card.

2. Press your thumb into a thin layer of tempera paint, then press it onto an index card. Press it several times until you can get the clearest print possible.

3. Lightly coat your thumb with olive oil just until your thumb feels slightly greasy. Be careful to not use too much. Press your thumb onto a mirror or glass. Try to keep your thumb as still as possible while pressing down and also when removing it in order to create the best print.

4. Lightly dust the greasy print you just left with baby powder and let it sit for a few minutes.

6. Finally, use tape to try and "lift" the print from the glass or mirror. Do this by carefully placing the piece of tape sticky side down on the print. Try your best to keep the tape from moving around as you press it down. Then lift it off the mirror starting at one end of the tape and pulling it slowly upwards.

CLASSIFYING FINGERPRINTS

Now that you have gathered your prints, see if you can classify them.
Fingerprints are classified into three major groups:

1. **Arch:** Ridges start from one end and extend to the other side.

Wikimedia Commons

2. **Whorl:** Ridges form a circular swirl in the center.

Wikimedia Commons

3. **Loop:** Ridges that start on one side, loop around, and flow back to the same side they started from. This is the most common type of fingerprint.

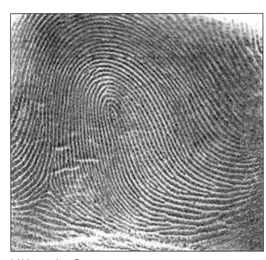

Wikimedia Commons

Using a magnifying glass, examine your fingerprints. Compare them with the fingerprint examples and classify yours.

Collecting Fingerprints

Sometimes there are fingerprints left at a crime scene that are easily visible. These are called *patent prints*. Just because an investigator may not see fingerprints, though, does not mean they are not there.

Latent prints are not visible to the naked eye. A fingerprint specialist uses colored powders to reveal these invisible prints. The oils from skin left on the print will cause the powder to stick to it. A magnetic brush is used to apply the powder so that the prints are not smeared. Once the fingerprints are revealed, they can be photographed and documented. Then they are taken to the lab and stored for trial. Some prints can be lifted with special tape. The sticky side is placed on the print and the investigator carefully lifts it off the surface.

Other prints may be harder to lift. Sometimes an object that the print is on can be taken back to the lab if the object is small enough, like a can. The can is then placed in a fume-filled box to reveal the print more dramatically. Cyanoacrylate adhesive (super glue) fumes are released inside the box, coating and sticking to the can. The print can then be dusted with a fluorescent powder and held under an alternate light source. Now the print will be clearly visible for the forensic examiner to study.

Dusting for fingerprints.
Wikimedia Commons

fingerprint discoveries. They were not interested. In fact, they were quite happy with the Bertillon system of identification.

About the same time Faulds was working with fingerprints, Sir William Herschel was making his own fingerprint discoveries in India. Herschel worked as a government official, and he required that documents be signed with palm prints by those who could not write. Herschel too began noticing the uniqueness of fingerprints. He also observed that even as people age, their fingerprints do not change.

Both Faulds and Herschel would argue about who should receive credit for discovering the value of fingerprints. It took another man, however, to take their findings a step further. A psychologist and anthropologist named Sir Francis Galton saw that fingerprinting could be useful in crime solving only if a method of classifying fingerprints could be developed. In 1892, he wrote a book titled *Fingerprints*, a scientific book with thorough studies. This book gave validity to the use of fingerprints as a means of identifying criminals and inspired other forensic minds. Galton also created a fingerprint classification method. It was a complicated system, though, and not practical for police officers to use.

ALL ABOARD HENRY'S SYSTEM

In order for fingerprints to be used in criminal investigation, there needed to be a classification system that was easy to use, unlike the Bertillon system. Sir Edward Henry, a police commissioner, sat on a train one day, contemplating such a system. It suddenly occurred to him how he could classify the fingerprints into a simple system, one that could be used by police officers everywhere. This classification method became known as the Henry Classification System.

In 1901, Henry became head of the Criminal Investigation Department at Scotland Yard. He also started the central fingerprint bureau there. The first time his work led to a conviction of a criminal occurred in 1902.

A home in London was burglarized and the perpetrator left fingerprints on a freshly painted windowsill. Henry's fingerprint bureau was called on to help and a detective from the bureau came and took a photograph of the print. He compared the photo with other fingerprints the bureau had on file and found that the prints matched those of a man named Harry Jackson, who had served time for burglary.

Investigators arrested Jackson and took new fingerprints from him. The new prints were photographed and blown up to a large size. The crime scene photos were also enlarged. Now jurors could easily view them both in court, side by side. Jurors were then taught Henry's fingerprint system to help them understand what they were looking at.

Even though Jackson was found guilty, a lot of people were skeptical of his conviction. Many people did not trust this unusual new fingerprint method. It seemed very strange to identify people from lines on their fingers. It took a while for Henry's fingerprint system to be accepted, but eventually it completely replaced the Bertillon system. It is actually the method of classification our current fingerprint system is based on today.

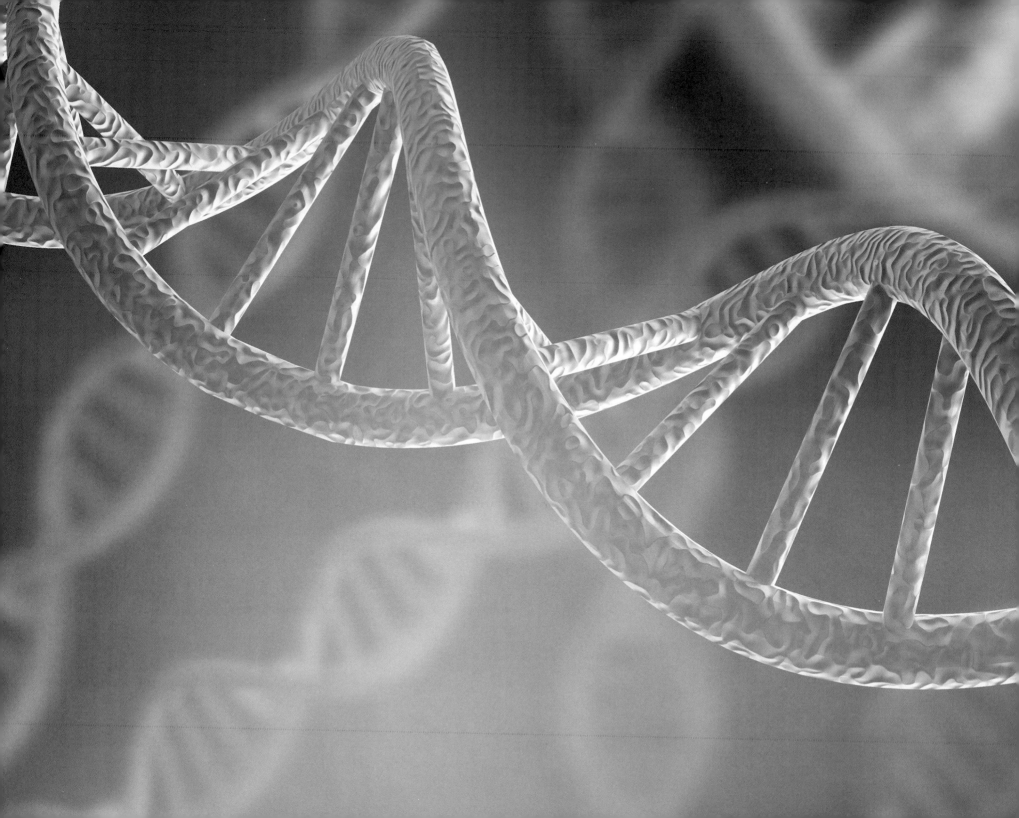

THE MANY FORMS OF IDENTIFICATION

Have you ever had x-rays taken of your teeth by a dentist? Not only do the x-rays reveal cavities, they also uncover the unique details of your teeth, like tooth shape. Forensic scientists can use teeth to help identify people, especially victims. Your teeth are the hardest substance in your body, even harder than your bones. In certain situations, teeth are the only remains left to help identify someone. Using dental science in investigations is called *forensic odontology*.

Hitler's Teeth

Realizing he was about to be defeated in World War II, Nazi leader Adolf Hitler died by suicide on April 30, 1945. His body was then burned, apparently the last order he gave. And while it seemed clear that the remains belonged to Hitler, what if they didn't? Rumors began surfacing suggesting that Hitler was alive and hiding somewhere, and that the charred remains were someone else's.

But forensic odontology was able to finally silence the rumors and prove that the burned corpse was that of Adolf Hitler. Hitler had horrible dental hygiene and had very few real teeth left. He could eat only soft vegetables. He had tooth decay, bridges, and dentures that were very distinct. Dental remains were compared with his dental records to prove that the burned corpse was most definitely that of Adolf Hitler.

EXTRA THE STARS AND STRIPES **EXTRA**

HITLER DEAD

Fuehrer Fell at CP, German Radio Says; Doenitz at Helm, Vows War Will Continue

Churchill Hints Peace Is at Hand

***Stars and Stripes*, the newspaper of the US Army, announces Hitler's death.**
Wikimedia Commons

One of the first identifications using odontology occurred in 1776 and involved a man you have probably heard of: Paul Revere. Apprenticed by his father as a silversmith, Revere was also trained as a dentist. He made a set of ivory dentures for Gen. Joseph Warren, the man who sent Revere on his midnight ride.

Back then, fake teeth were actually wired to existing teeth inside a person's mouth. When General Warren was killed at the Battle of Bunker Hill, his body was buried in a mass grave with other soldiers. Nine months later, when the grave was unearthed, the decomposed bodies were unrecognizable. But Revere was able to identify Warren's body by the teeth he had created for him.

Unfortunately, sometimes it takes tragedy to push forensics forward. This was the case with odontology. In 1887, a yearly charity bazaar was held in Paris. The large building filled with people. It was a happy occasion with many important aristocrats from the United States as well as Europe. A fire started and spread quickly in the wooden structure. Tragically, 126 people, mostly women, died, and 150 more were injured.

Three dentists assisted in identifying many of the victims. Although Dr. Amoedo, a dentist and professor, was not one of them, he was profoundly affected by the disaster. He interviewed the dentists who had served in the aftermath. He realized a book was needed for dentists to assist them in forensic odontology. In his book, Amoedo developed standard methods of using odontology

Odontology

Odontology includes not only dental records but also bite marks. Sometimes, bite marks are found at a crime scene in a piece of food, like an apple. If investigators can match the marks to a suspect, they will have a strong piece of evidence. See if you can match the bite marks.

You'll Need

- 2 volunteers
- 2 Styrofoam plates folded in half
- paper towels
- 2 cheese slices, each folded in half
- 2 slices of bread, each folded in half
- an apple cut in half
- paper
- colored permanent markers

1. In this activity, you will try to match each plate bite mark with the correct cheese, apple, and bread slice bite marks. First, give two people a plate, cheese slice, bread slice, and apple slice. Then leave the room until they have prepared the bite samples.

2. While you are gone, each person should bite into a Styrofoam plate and label it A or B. Then, they will bite into their cheese slice, apple slice, and bread slice. Mark each sample with a different color permanent marker—six different colors. They will record the colors they used for each sample on a piece of paper so that they do not forget. Next, they will lay out their six samples on a paper towel, mixing them together.

3. Using disposable gloves, take each set of Styrofoam plate bites and examine them using a magnifying glass or microscope. Do you see any unusual markings? Make a note of your findings for each different bite sample.

4. Now examine the cheese slices, apple slices, and bread slices. See if you can determine which bite marks match which plate bite and record your findings.

5. Check with your friends to see if you matched them correctly.

for identification. Because of this important work, he became known as the father of odontology.

Did you know that your body has more than 200 bones? Your bones contain clues to what you look like, your age, height, sex, ethnicity, and even what you eat. An arthritic hand or pointed jaw are individual bone characteristics that can help identify someone. Scientists who study human bones for the purpose of identification are called *forensic anthropologists*.

Anthropology entered the forensic stage in 1894. That is when a Harvard medical professor named Thomas Dwight began writing research articles and essays. His writing shined a spotlight on the science of human skeletal identification. He even created seminars to teach others, earning him the title of father of forensic anthropology.

Lectures were one thing, but two wars made it clear how important skeletal remains are in identification. After World War II, many soldiers' badly decomposed bodies could not be identified. Families desperately needed their loved ones identified for closure and proper burials. The Central Identification Lab was created in Hawaii to help.

Geologist and anthropologist Charles E. Snow was assigned to lead it. When he left to return to his teaching position, another leader was sought. Mildred Trotter was chosen. Trotter was the first woman professor of gross anatomy at the Washington University School of Medicine. Along with helping to identify soldiers' remains, Trotter developed important research. She created formulas for measuring the long bones of skeletal remains to determine a person's height. Her formulas are still used today.

Another identification lab was set up in Japan during the Korean War (1950–1953). This time, T. Dale Stewart, an anthropologist from the

Grave Robbers

Medical and scientific discoveries are the backbone of forensic science. Understanding human anatomy has proven invaluable in solving crimes, finding criminals, and identifying victims.

Unusual measures to study the human anatomy took place in the 1700s. Medical professors and students realized they needed real human corpses to study in order to truly gain knowledge in medicine, especially in the area of surgery. There were few corpses available to examine, though. Occasionally, the body of an executed offender was given to a medical university, but that was not often.

Some medical schools began to hire men to steal corpses from new graves. They would pay robbers, called *resurrection men*, for the corpses. Harvard medical students started a group called the Spunker Club. Members decided to dig up graves themselves instead of paying resurrection men. People were obviously outraged, especially those whose loved one's graves had been robbed. Finally, in 1815, Massachusetts made it a felony to steal a body from a grave.

In 1999, evidence of the strange spree of grave robbing in our history was found at Harvard University. During construction work, many skeletal remains were uncovered behind a wall in Harvard's Holden Chapel. This was the building where anatomy lessons were held during the first years of Harvard's medical school.

Smithsonian Institution, was asked to direct it. With the success of these two identification labs, it became easier to see how beneficial anthropology could be in criminal investigations. Finally, in the 1970s, forensic anthropology became an official branch of forensics.

CLYDE SNOW, FORENSIC ANTHROPOLOGIST

Dr. Clyde Snow (1928–2014) is perhaps the most famous forensic anthropologist in the world. He helped to identify hundreds of skeletal remains in many places all over the globe. Dr. Snow was born in a small Texas town called Ralls in 1928, but he eventually made his home in Oklahoma. Among the many fields he studied was archaeology. In 1955, he earned a master's degree in zoology and studied rhesus monkeys in Peru. Later, he completed his PhD in anthropology.

Snow began working for the Federal Aviation Administration (FAA) in Oklahoma City in 1960. There, he worked on research to make flights safer. On the side, he helped identify skeletal remains, establishing himself as one of the few forensic anthropologists at the time.

In 1979, the tragic crash of American Airlines Flight 191 in Chicago killed 271 people onboard and 2 others on the ground. Snow was asked to help identify the victims. After that, his expertise became more and more sought after. He worked on many local and national homicide cases, helping identify victims and solving cases.

One of the more well-known cases he worked on was the reexamination of President John F. Kennedy's assassination. He also helped identify victims in the Oklahoma City bombing in 1995. In 2006, he testified for hours in the trial of Iraqi dictator Saddam Hussein. Hussein had ordered the brutal torture and killing of his own people before and during the Iraq War.

In 1985, Snow was asked to help identify skeletal remains of thousands of people in unmarked graves in Argentina. Under ruthless political leaders, many people had been killed. Their families were told they had simply disappeared. When new leadership emerged, families wanted to know where their loved ones' bodies were buried and what had happened to them. Argentinian authorities asked the American Association for the Advancement of Science for help. Snow was invited to be part of the team.

What he thought would only last a few weeks ended up lasting several years. While in Argentina, he and his team trained Argentinian anthropology students. They also took part in bringing some of the military leaders to justice for the horrible atrocities they had committed.

"[Bones] don't forget and they always tell the truth," Snow would tell his students. "They speak so softly, you have to use your eyes to listen to them rather than your ears."

Snow traveled to many other countries, including Peru, Iraq, and Brazil, where he served in similar humanitarian efforts and trained students. He believed it was extremely important for forensic scientists to be involved in humanitarian concerns.

Anthropologist William R. Maples

William Maples (1937–1997) earned his PhD in anthropology in 1967 and then began teaching at several universities in the United States. Investigators and medical examiners soon recognized his expertise and asked for his help with cases and identifications of victims. Maples ended up working on more than 1,000 cases, and some of them were quite well known.

One of the most famous cases he worked on was the identification of skeletal remains discovered in Russia. He and his team concluded that the bones belonged to five members of the Romanov family who had been executed in 1918. Later, DNA testing confirmed that their findings were correct.

In 1991, the body of President Zachary Taylor was exhumed in order to determine if the rumors about the cause of his death were truth or fiction. Many people believed Taylor had been murdered in 1850 because of his antislavery stance. The ability to prove if Taylor's stomach pains and then sudden death were from arsenic did not exist when he died. Maples thought it was important to know for certain if an American president had been murdered or not. But after Maples conducted the examination, he concluded that Taylor had died of gastroenteritis, an infection of the digestive system, not arsenic poisoning.

In another case, with Maples's help, the person responsible for the death of civil rights leader Medgar Evers was finally brought to justice. In 1963, Evers was shot and killed. Thirty years later, Maples and his team analyzed Evers's exhumed remains. They found enough forensic evidence to convict a Ku Klux Klan member, Byron De La Beckwith, with his murder.

In the 1970s, Maples worked at the Central Identification Lab in Hawaii. There, he helped identify US soldiers' remains from the Vietnam War and other US conflicts.

In another famous case, Maples solved the unusual mystery of Joseph Merrick, also known as the "Elephant Man." Merrick suffered from a disfiguring disease that caused an overgrowth of his bones and skin. He led a sad and lonely life, never able to fit into regular society. Medical professionals speculated as to what might have caused his disfigurement, but no one knew for sure. Then in 1998, Maples examined Merrick's skeletal remains and concluded that he suffered from a rare disease called Proteus syndrome.

The Romanov family, 1913. *Wikimedia Commons*

"I'm anti-homicide, no matter who it happens to or where it occurs. I think homicide is the greatest violation of human rights that can be committed."

In 1985, Snow was asked to help examine a skeleton in Brazil. It was believed to belong to Josef Mengele, also called the "Angel of Death." Mengele was a Nazi war criminal. He had helped kill and torture thousands of people, mostly Jews in the Auschwitz concentration camp during Hitler's regime. Mengele had been living in hiding after the war.

Snow and his team concluded the bones were almost certainly the bones of Josef Mengele. A few years later, a DNA test confirmed that their findings were correct. Investigations revealed that Mengele had died by drowning.

FORENSICS IN RWANDA

Snow's trip to Argentina was the first time that forensic anthropology had been used in a human rights mission. It inspired a 23-year-old woman named Clea Koff to join another human rights endeavor in 1996 in Rwanda, in Africa.

Koff was an anthropology graduate student and joined the team assigned the job of unearthing a mass grave containing hundreds of corpses. The people of Rwanda had experienced horrible genocide in 1994. One group called the Hutu had massacred mostly people from another group called the Tutsi. More than 800,000 individuals were violently killed. Koff and the other team members had to piece together skeletal bones and identify

victims. Then the bodies could be returned to their families and properly buried.

The process of identification involved asking a series of questions. What ethnicity did this person belong to? Were they male or female, and how old were they? By examining the skulls, bones, and teeth, anthropologists answered these questions. All this information was pieced together with clothing and other personal items found with the victims, and this helped clarify their identities. Often DNA samples from bones were compared to live family members' DNA to further back up their findings.

Temporary labs were set up in tents for x-rays and autopsies as needed. The forensic team did not just identify the victims but acquired the evidence needed to prove genocide so that the perpetrators could be brought to justice.

Koff went on to join forensic anthropology teams in other countries with similar cases. She eventually wrote a book about her experiences in Rwanda titled *The Bone Woman*.

LOTS OF BONES

There are many anthropology labs that help with investigations. One of the most well-known anthropology labs is the Smithsonian Department of Anthropology. It is located in the National Museum of Natural History in Washington, DC. Anthropologists there work with the FBI and other law enforcement agencies to help solve crimes.

The Smithsonian also contains thousands of human skeletal remains that represent

Skeletal Identification

Forensic anthropologists learn how to analyze skeletal remains in order to determine an individual's identity. Four main aspects they seek to learn first are the ethnicity, sex, age, and height. Learning this information can help the anthropologist place the bones in a smaller category. Then they can work from there to determine who the individual is.

ETHNICITY

There are many diverse ethnic groups of people in our world. Narrowing down the group to which a victim belongs can clarify his or her identity. Examining the skull is helpful in determining this. While there are always exceptions, generally speaking, there are several differences. Asian skulls are usually wider with more distinct cheekbones. The eye orbits (bony area that houses the eyes) are circular, and nasal openings are slightly heart shaped. European skulls tend to be long and narrow with sharp angles and circular eye orbits. African skulls have more rectangular eye orbits and wider nasal openings.

A reconstructed skull used for evidence.
American Association for the Advancement of Science

MALE OR FEMALE

Placing found bones in the biological female or male group is very helpful for the forensic anthropologist in determining identify. Males tend to have larger, thicker bones in general. The pelvis bone in a female is also wider. A female's skull is rounder and smoother. The male jaw is usually more square than the female jaw. Males also have more of a distinct brow ridge and their foreheads slope backward.

HEIGHT

Forensic anthropologists use a mathematical formula to determine height. There are different calculations used for different genders as well as different ethnicities. Each calculation, however, uses the same basic formula that contains the length of a skeleton's long bones, such as the femur (thigh bone) or humerus (upper-arm bone).

AGE

Forensic anthropologists know how bones develop. This knowledge helps them determine age. For instance, children's bones are not fused together yet, and those of young adults under age 25 are only partially fused. Understanding the degeneration process of aging helps anthropologists determine the age of older adults. Teeth are also helpful in age identification.

populations all over the world. This collection is a valuable source for training anthropologists and for research. The Smithsonian also receives skeleton donations from the Body Farm in Tennessee.

The Body Farm is a wooded area near Knoxville, Tennessee, where corpses are donated for research. The only way to really understand how the human body decomposes is to observe the process as it happens. That is why anthropologist William Bass created the Body Farm in 1987.

Forensic students and professionals come from all over the country to learn about the decomposition of corpses at the Body Farm. They study how corpses decay under many different conditions. The Body Farm has been so effective in forensic training that now there are several more body farms in other areas throughout the United States.

THE CENTER FOR HUMAN IDENTIFICATION

A staggering number of people are reported missing each year in the United States, close to 600,000. Thankfully, most of them are later located. Tens of thousands of them, however, remain missing after one year. There are also more than 4,000 unidentified bodies found each year. Sadly, approximately 1,000 of them still remain unidentified after one year.

The University of North Texas Center for Human Identification (UNTCHI) is a forensic lab dedicated to helping authorities identify human remains and missing persons. The lab is located at the University of North Texas Health Science Center in Fort Worth, Texas. UNTCHI is one of about 200 labs approved to access the national DNA database called CODIS.

In criminal investigations, forensic testing is sometimes required on skeletal remains for identification. Fifty percent of the time, authorities have a good idea of who the remains belong to. Investigators often accompany the unknown bone sample with known evidence samples for comparison to see if their hunch is correct. Forensic analysts at UNTCHI grind a small amount of the bone sample into powder in order to collect DNA. They then perform analysis to see if the DNA matches the known sample of the suspected individual.

Other cases might involve found remains similar to the bones found in the Bering Sea in 2009. Alaskan fishermen on the *Blue Gadus* discovered three human bones stuck in their fishing net after they pulled it aboard. Later, an anthropologist confirmed that the bones belonged to a single individual. Samples from the bones were sent 4,000 miles away to the UNTCHI forensic lab. There, forensic scientists took a DNA sample from the bones and submitted it in the CODIS database.

Within the CODIS database there are several categories of DNA types. The UNTCHI has access to some DNA files that other labs are not approved to access. One of these is the mitochondrial DNA category. Mitochondrial DNA is passed down from the biological mother. Very few US labs are approved to access this DNA group.

The mitochondrial DNA of the Bering Sea bones matched with Kathy Meincke, whose DNA was submitted to CODIS 14 years earlier. The bones belonged to her son, Jeff Meincke. He was 20 years old when he died on a fishing boat called the *Arctic Rose* in 2001. The ship sank, killing all 15 crew members, but only the captain's remains had previously been found.

In the case of missing persons, forensic scientists at UNTCHI utilize the missing persons category within the CODIS database. A DNA sample from a missing person's family member—like Kathy Meincke's—is often added to this category at some point. Sometimes, personal materials belonging to the missing person are submitted to UNTCHI in order to obtain DNA. Examples are a toothbrush or dentures. The DNA codes in the missing persons file are constantly compared with the file of unknown remains to see if there is a match. Sometimes there is, while other times there is not. The missing person might actually still be alive somewhere, or the remains may simply not have been found yet.

EVERY SKULL HAS A FACE

Sometimes, even with all the information an anthropologist obtains from examining a skeleton, the person may still remain unidentified. When this happens, it may be time to put a face on the remains. This is done by a forensic artist, who reconstructs the face from the skull.

A plastic copy of the skull is made first for the artist to build on. Using modeling clay, the forensic artist forms the head and face on top of the plastic copy. An anthropologist who has studied the original skull provides a report that helps guide the artist. This report contains valuable information concerning the race, sex, and age of the unidentified person. Details of the scene where

How a face is "reconstructed" from a skull. *FBI*

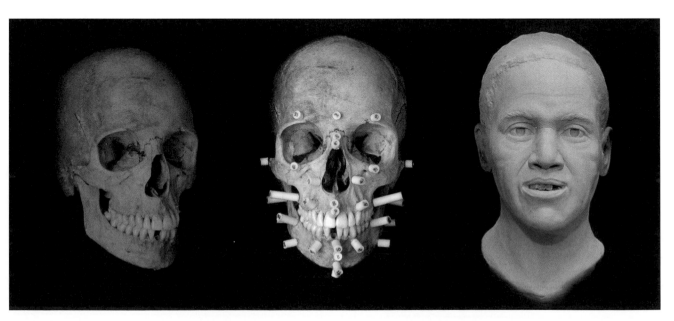

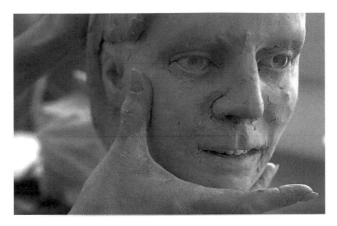

A forensic artist reconstructs a face. *FBI*

the skeleton was found might also prove helpful.

The artist places pegs on the skull that note the different thicknesses of soft tissue on different areas of the face. Layers of tissue and muscle are slowly built up with clay. The artist smooths the "skin" on top, refining the nose, ears, and eyes. Sometimes there are clues about the hair given on the anthropologist's report. Sometimes the artist must guess. The idea is to create a face that closely resembles the individual. It will not be an exact replica.

Computer software programs are now often used to recreate a face from a skull. The skull is scanned into a computer and merged with a CT scan of a living person's face. The CT scan contains the tissue and muscle information. The skull is matched with a face that is in close proximity to the age, sex, and ethnicity contained in the anthropologist's report. The tissue and muscles from the live face are merged into the digitized image of the skull. A specialist can then finish the details on the computerized face.

Frank Bender:
Facial Reconstruction Artist

For many years, Frank Bender (1941–2011) worked as a forensic artist, helping law enforcement solve crimes. He helped to put identifiable faces on victims of crime and also on wanted criminals. Police departments, the FBI, and Scotland Yard were among the many law enforcement agencies he served.

His first career was not in crime solving, though. He started out as a commercial photographer. Along the way, he became interested in human anatomy. His passion for learning led him to study actual bodies in a morgue. Eventually, he was given the job of creating a ceramic head and face (bust) from the skull of a murder victim that was never identified. It was a success. The victim, Anna Duvall, was recognized from Bender's reconstruction.

Before long, he left the photography business and became a fine artist and forensic artist. In 1989, he was asked to assist a television show called *America's Most Wanted*. On this show, fugitives on the run were highlighted in hopes that someone watching the show would recognize them. Bender was asked to create a bust of a man named John Emil List, who had killed his family 18 years earlier. Bender would need to make the face look 18 years older than the available photographs of the killer.

Within a short time of the program being aired, a woman recognized the face as that of a neighbor in Denver, Colorado, who went by a different name. A few weeks later, List was arrested by FBI agents and eventually sentenced to life in prison. Bender's sculpture was a success.

Bender also helped start an organization called the Vidocq Society named after Eugène François Vidocq, an 1800s detective. The Vidocq Society is a group of forensic experts who help assist law enforcement departments in solving cold cases.

Clay Face Reconstruction

Imagine that you are just like Frank Bender, one of the top forensic reconstruction artists in the nation. A construction company has found a skull while laying a foundation for a tall building. It could be centuries old! You have been called on to reconstruct it.

You'll Need

- 🔎 small plastic skull (can be found at a craft store or online)
- 🔎 air-dry clay
- 🔎 black marker
- 🔎 rolling pin
- 🔎 plastic knife
- 🔎 water
- 🔎 craft sticks

ANTHROPOLOGIST'S REPORT:

- 🔎 Male between the ages of 30 and 35
- 🔎 Wide cheekbones
- 🔎 Oval-shaped face
- 🔎 High forehead
- 🔎 Short, wide nose

1. Cover the whole skull in a thin layer of clay, smoothing it with your hands. This represents the thinnest layer of tissue.

2. Roll out the clay into thin slabs for the second layer. Using a plastic knife, cut the clay into strips and add more thickness where needed such as the cheeks, chin and forehead.

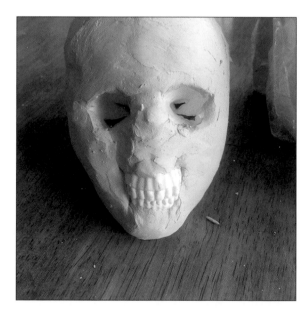

3. Add strips and pieces of clay to form the nose, lips, and brow. Add more strips for the cheek bones and high forehead and build up the nose as needed to match the anthropologist's report as closely as you can. Roll up balls of clay and place them in the skull's sockets to form eyes.

4. Read the anthropologist's report again and make any last adjustments if needed.

EVERY FACE HAS A NAME

When a crime has been committed, a witness or victim will try to describe the criminal to authorities. This can be a difficult task, especially if emotions are heightened. A forensic artist is trained to talk with traumatized witnesses or victims to help them describe the perpetrator. This image can be compared with pictures of known offenders. It can also be shown to the public in the hopes that someone will recognize him or her.

In 1995, a truck that was parked outside the Alfred P. Murrah Federal Building in Oklahoma City exploded. One hundred sixty-eight people died. Hundreds more were injured. Forensic professionals, including anthropologists, helped to identify the victims' remains. The hunt was on for the culprit who had committed the horrible crime. That's where the help of a forensic sketch artist came in.

Remains of the explosive truck were linked to a rental company in Kansas. Employees from the rental company gave an FBI sketch artist a description of the man who had rented the vehicle. The sketch was shared with people in the surrounding area. A motel owner recognized the drawing of the man. She said he had rented a room in her motel under the name of Timothy McVeigh. Fortunately, McVeigh was easy to find: he was already in jail in Oklahoma for a traffic violation. He was found guilty and executed in 2001.

Now, there are computer software programs that can help design images of suspects. Many police departments do not have trained artists who can create composite drawings, but officers can be trained to use computer programs.

These programs are filled with different-shaped faces, different facial features such as eyes and mouths, even different hairstyles and glasses. The trained officer can use the program to create the face the witness describes. Witnesses can tell the officer what needs to be changed or altered until they are content with the created likeness.

IDENTIFYING BLOOD

In the 1800s, no one had the ability to determine if a dried substance that looked like blood was actually blood—except, of course, for Sherlock Holmes. In the first crime novel, Holmes had a remarkable test that could determine if a substance was blood. In the real world, a dried red substance found at a crime scene could be any number of things—perhaps paint, sauce, or dye.

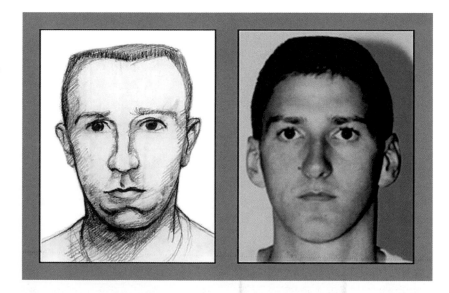

The composite drawing that led authorities to Timothy McVeigh. *FBI*

In 1853, a physician named Ludwig Teichmann created a test that could determine if hemin was present in a questionable stain. Hemin is a crystalline substance that forms when blood dries. If hemin was found, investigators knew it was blood. The test was called the *Teichmann test*, and it is still used in investigations today as a presumptive test.

A presumptive test is an initial test done on evidence to see if further testing is necessary. If the Teichmann test reveals that a stain is blood, then it is sent to a forensic lab for further testing. If the Teichmann test shows that the substance is not blood, then investigators know they do not need to waste time on further testing.

The Teichmann test was a big breakthrough in the 1800s, but a suspect could still claim that the blood discovered on his clothes was from an animal. Many people lived on farms and ranches, and animal blood would not be unusual. A test was needed that could prove not only that a stain was blood but that it was human blood.

Then in 1891, a professor in Germany named Paul Uhlenhuth devised the **precipitin test.** This test could distinguish if blood was from a human or an animal.

Uhlenhuth's test was developed from his experiments with animal blood. He took the part of the blood called *serum* from rabbits and noticed that clumps appeared if the serum was mixed with human blood. When he mixed the serum with other animal blood, it did not clump. Now investigators could use this test to learn if blood was from a human.

Composite Drawing

Imagine you are a police sketch artist. A witness (friend) has seen a suspect flee from the scene of a burglary. Now the witness will describe the suspect to you as you draw the face.

You'll Need

- volunteer
- drawing paper
- pencil
- magazine with a picture of a face

1. Ask your friend (witness) to look at a picture of a face in a magazine and describe it to you.

2. During your interview with the witness, ask specific questions that will help you create an accurate drawing.

3. Sketch a face according to the description.

4. When you have completed the drawing, compare it with the magazine picture. Do you think your drawing would help police find the suspect?

Blood Pattern Analysis

Sometimes bloodstains are left at a crime scene. The patterns made by the stains are a written story of what has happened, which a bloodstain analyst is trained to read. The bloodstains are first photographed to record the exact details before any samples are collected. Then the examiner studies and measures them.

The three main groups of bloodstain patterns are *passive*, *transfer*, and *impact*. *Passive stains* are those that have dropped and created round stains. *Transfer patterns* occur when blood swipes against another material, smudging it. *Impact stains* are oval-shaped patterns formed by a force that has propelled the blood through the air.

Each type of pattern can be measured by the forensic analyst and calculated to determine certain types of information. Using science and math, the examiner learns the distance the blood traveled from the wound and the angle and type of force used. How many people were involved, what type of weapon was used, and the action of the characters all become clear to the forensic analyst.

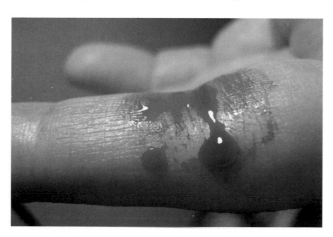

Human blood traces can be used to identify victims and criminals.
Wikimedia Commons

Suspects could still claim the blood was their own, though, and not that of a victim. Perhaps the stain was from a cut hand or a nosebleed. How could investigators determine if the human blood found at a scene or on a piece of clothing belonged to a specific person? This was the next dilemma.

BLOOD TYPES

Blood transfusions are conducted when a person has lost dangerous amounts of blood, perhaps through a traumatic event, such as a car accident. The patient is given blood from another person through a tube and needle in his or her arm. In the 1900s, blood transfusions were often unsuccessful, but no one understood why patients sometimes died.

Austrian physician Karl Landsteiner experimented with blood to try and learn the answer. He discovered that each person's blood can be classified into different types, which today we know as A, AB, B, or O. So the problem was that not everyone had the same type of blood!

Blood typing was a huge help in criminal investigations. Even though a specific individual could not be identified this way, the process could at least narrow down the list of suspects.

UNIQUELY YOU

There is one type of identification that outshines them all. Alec Jeffreys discovered DNA fingerprinting in 1984. His work finally solved the mystery scientists before him had been uncovering bits and pieces of.

It started in 1869, when Friedrich Miescher came across a curious substance in the nucleus of blood cells. He did not realize it, but he had discovered DNA. DNA is short for *deoxyribonucleic acid*. DNA contains information much like a computer program or barcode on a store item. This information is basically the program of each individual.

Scientists James Watson and Francis Crick built on Miescher's discovery and learned more about DNA. They discovered that DNA is shaped like a twisted ladder called a *double helix*. What Jeffreys found was that the coding contained in the DNA ladder is unique to each individual.

No one who has ever lived or ever will live contains the exact same DNA coding as you. The 10 trillion cells in your body contain your unique program. Because of DNA analysis, forensic scientists today can identify a specific individual from a tiny amount of blood, tissue, hair, or even saliva.

A year after making his discovery, Jeffreys had the opportunity to use it in an investigation. Police asked for his help in solving a recent murder not far from Jeffreys's lab. They believed the perpetrator also killed another person in the same general area three years earlier. They had no leads until one man named George Howard said he had committed the second murder but not the first.

Jeffreys collected DNA samples from fluid found on each victim's body that did not belong to the victims themselves. He compared the two DNA samples with that of George Howard. They did not match Howard's DNA, but Jeffreys learned that the same person had definitely committed both crimes. He knew this because the DNA from both fluid samples was the same. Now police knew Howard was not the killer, but they also knew they were searching for only one suspect.

Police believed the perpetrator was still in the area. They set up testing sites at hospitals where all men between the ages of 17 and 34 were urged to give blood samples for Jeffreys to test. Police also went into remote areas setting up temporary blood centers to make sure everyone was tested. Over 4,000 men gave blood samples. Authorities could not legally order anyone to give blood, but innocent people wanted to comply. They wanted the murderer to be found. Police knew the criminal would try to avoid giving blood, but hopefully someone would notice and turn him in.

Eight months later, a group of bakery workers were relaxing in a pub and one of the workers shared some interesting information with the others. He told them that his friend Colin Pitchfork had talked him into taking the blood test in his place. The information was shared with the police and they arrested Pitchfork. When Jeffreys tested Pitchfork's DNA, he found that it matched the samples from the victims' bodies. Pitchfork was tried and convicted.

Suddenly, police and investigators everywhere wanted to learn how to use this new DNA identification method. Forensic science would never be the same.

Alec Jeffreys.
Jane Gitschier, Wikimedia Commons

4 MODERN FORENSICS MOVES FORWARD

If you went back in time to visit Edmond Locard's first forensic lab in the early 1900s, you would find very few examination tools—perhaps just a basic microscope and magnifying glass.

Locard's first attic room lab has now grown into sophisticated labs worldwide. These labs are filled with equipment that scientists like Locard could only dream of. One of the most valuable tools in a forensic lab continues to be the microscope. While there are many different types of microscopes available today, the comparison microscope is especially valuable to a forensic scientist.

LET'S COMPARE

Chemist Philip O. Gravelle designed the comparison microscope in the 1920s. It is basically two microscopes connected by one optical bridge. The left eyepiece views the item on the left stage, while the right eyepiece views what sits on the right stage. This makes it much simpler to compare two pieces of evidence at once.

Gravelle, with the help of his friend Calvin Goddard, developed this microscope for the purpose of studying firearm evidence such as bullets.

In most guns, a bullet sits inside a metal tube called a *cartridge casing.* When the trigger is pulled, the casing and bullet spin inside the gun barrel, moving forward. After the bullet releases from the barrel, the cartridge casing falls to the ground. Grooves inside the gun barrel create slight marks on the bullet and the cartridge casing as they turn inside when shot.

Each type of firearm creates a unique set of marks called *striations.* Forensic experts can study the cartridge casings and/or bullets found at a crime scene and learn what type of gun they were shot from. They can use a comparison microscope to study the striations on a bullet found at a crime scene and compare it with marks on a bullet fired from a suspected gun to see if they match.

THE CHICAGO MOB

Firearm crimes increased rapidly in the early 1900s. In response, Goddard, Gravelle, and others created a ballistics lab in New York called the Bureau of Forensic Ballistics. Ballistics is the study of firearms. Goddard became so well known for his assistance to investigators that he was asked to start a ballistics lab in Chicago.

In the 1920s, Chicago was overrun with violent crime. Organized criminal groups were centralized there and creating havoc. The biggest and most powerful one was referred to as the Mafia, or Mob. It was run by a ruthless killer named Al Capone.

One of the most famous cases Goddard helped Chicago police with involved Capone and his gang.

Every bullet has its own unique "fingerprint." *iStock/zoka74*

Toolmark Examiner

A tool examiner analyzes marks made on surfaces at a crime scene. Perhaps a window was pried open with a tool. An examiner can discover what kind of tool made the mark and sometimes even trace it to one unique tool. In this activity, you are the tool examiner who will test indented marks, abrasion marks, and hard surface marks.

You'll Need

- Styrofoam plates
- piece of wood
- cardboard
- Phillips-head screwdriver and flathead screwdriver
- large screw
- pliers
- magnifying glass
- volunteers

1. Lay out the wood, cardboard, and Styrofoam.

2. One at a time, make three test scratches on each surface using the screwdrivers, screw, pliers, and wrench. First, make an abrasion mark by lightly scratching the surface with each tool.

3. Next, make a cutting mark by pressing the tool across the surface.

4. Finally, make an indentation mark with each tool by pressing the object into the surface; try pressing the sides of the tool into the surface as well as the point of the tool.

5. Allow some friends to examine the marks with magnification. See if they can determine which tool made each mark, and explain why they made the choices they did. How accurate were they?

In the 1920s, it was illegal nationwide to produce and sell alcoholic beverages. Criminal gangs like Capone's made lots of money by illegally producing and selling huge quantities of alcohol. Rival gang leader George Moran, known as "Bugs," started stealing some of Capone's shipments of alcohol. Capone learned that one of his stolen shipments was going to be delivered to Moran's

General Jackson's Arm

One of the first cases in which ballistics was used in a death investigation occurred in 1863 when General "Stonewall" Jackson died. Gen. Thomas J. Jackson had just led his Confederate troops through a winning battle in Chancellorsville, Virginia, against the Union. When it was night, he and a few of his men rode out into the dark to assess their position. Suddenly, Jackson was hit by three musket balls, two in his left arm and one in his right hand.

Jackson was taken to a Confederate field hospital about five miles away. First, the musket balls were removed. Then, the doctor realized that Jackson's left arm was too shattered to save, so it was amputated. The general was then transported to a small building near a train station, with plans to board a train to Richmond, Virginia. He contracted pneumonia, though, and died eight days after the removal of his arm.

Jackson's arm was buried in a nearby family cemetery out of respect. The musket balls were kept for a later investigation. Witnesses told investigators that the shots came from Jackson's own men, who were confused and thought they were firing at enemy soldiers.

How could investigators be sure the witnesses were correct? After all, it was too dark for anyone to see clearly and know if enemy shots had also been fired.

Investigators needed another way to determine who had shot Jackson. At that time, the Union soldiers had long-barreled muskets. These barrels had rifling, or grooves that created marks on the musket balls as they traveled through the barrels. The Confederate army's muskets were short barreled without rifling, so the bullets shot from their muskets were smooth. Investigators could easily see that the musket balls removed from Jackson's arm were smooth, proving that Jackson was in fact shot by friendly Confederate fire.

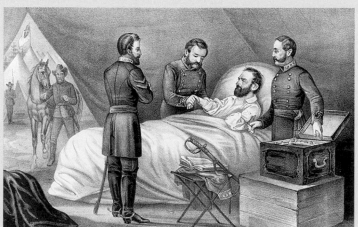

The Death of "Stonewall" Jackson. *Library of Congress (LC-DIG-pga-08551)*

warehouse on Valentine's Day, but Capone had plans of his own.

On February 14, 1929, the Moran gang arrived at the warehouse. Capone's thugs drove up in a vehicle that looked like a police car. The men, who were dressed like police officers, went inside. Moran arrived late and saw what he thought was police and left the scene. Moran's gang believed the men were police too. They lined up against the wall and laid their guns on the floor as they were ordered to, waiting to be arrested. But Capone's gang opened fire, killing Moran's men, and then fled the scene.

Police found more than 30 bullets and even more shell casings at the crime scene for Goddard to examine. He knew that the ammunition came from automatic submachine guns. After examining the marks on the shell casings, he learned that there were two types of marks. He concluded that at least two guns had been used and that the guns were Thompson submachine guns, also called tommy guns.

At the time, the Chicago police possessed tommy guns, and some questioned if they were the weapons used in the murders. After comparing bullets from police guns with the crime scene bullets, Goddard was able to prove that the bullets were not shot from the police guns. Investigators needed to find the weapons in order to link them to the real killers.

Ten months later, police officers found two tommy guns in the home of a man named Fred Burke. Burke was one of Capone's mobsters. He was already on the loose after shooting a police

Al Capone's FBI file.
Wikimedia Commons

officer while escaping arrest for another crime. Goddard was able to analyze the tommy guns and determine that they were in fact the weapons used in the massacre.

Burke was eventually found, tried for the murder of the police officer, and sentenced to life in prison. He died a few years later, never brought to trial for the St. Valentine's Day murders. Eventually, Capone and Moran were convicted of other crimes.

THE FBI

Chicago wasn't the only city wrestling with mounting crime. Across the nation, more and more people were moving into cities to find work. Overcrowded factories along with poorly paid immigrants created a tense atmosphere, which led to violence. Gangs similar to Al Capone's slithered in and sometimes found corrupt police they could partner with.

Criminal behavior among politicians, business owners, and other leaders was much more than local police departments could handle. As if that wasn't enough, organized groups referred to as *anarchists* were busy as well. They developed terrorist tactics such as assassinations and arson that fueled fear.

In 1908, under President Theodore Roosevelt, the Federal Bureau of Investigation (FBI) was formed to help with dangerous criminal activity nationwide. However, there was no lab to assist in a scientific way.

After the St. Valentine's Day Massacre, Goddard started the Scientific Crime Detection Lab in Chicago, where he offered forensic training for investigators. FBI agent and scientist Charles Appel attended classes at Goddard's lab and returned with a desire to start the first FBI crime lab.

In 1932, with President Herbert Hoover's permission, Appel and fellow agents set up the FBI lab in only one room. Today, the FBI Lab is one of the largest crime labs in the world. It is located on Marine Corps Base in Quantico, Virginia, and has more than 400 employees. There are also hundreds of other smaller forensic labs that are now all over the world.

The FBI Lab. *FBI*

INVESTIGATING PRESIDENT JOHN F. KENNEDY'S ASSASSINATION

When President John F. Kennedy was assassinated on November 22, 1963, Americans were shocked and horrified. Kennedy was shot and killed while riding in an open-top limousine as he waved to crowds in downtown Dallas, Texas. His friend, Governor John Connally, riding with him, was also shot and wounded.

A man named Lee Harvey Oswald was believed to have fired the deadly shots. He was taken into custody shortly after the shooting and charged with the murder of Kennedy and the murder of a police officer who had questioned him.

As Oswald was ushered out of a city jail to a more secure county jail, he was shot and killed by a man named Jack Ruby. Ruby, a night club operator, claimed he shot Oswald out of anger and disgust over the president's murder.

Many did not accept Ruby's story. They believed that Ruby wanted to silence Oswald so he could not expose the criminals he had conspired with to kill President Kennedy.

Vice President Lyndon Johnson was sworn in as the new president. On November 29, 1963, he organized a commission to investigate Kennedy's assassination. This commission, called the Warren Commission, was led by Supreme Court Chief Justice Earl Warren.

The yearlong investigation included an investigation of the crime scene, witness testimonies, acoustic studies, ballistics, autopsy findings, and fingerprints. The Warren Commission finally concluded that Oswald had fired three shots from a rifle and that the third shot had ended the president's life. The commission believed Oswald had acted alone without conspiring with other individuals or groups. The commission determined he had fired the shots from the sixth floor of the Texas School Book Depository building.

The Warren Commission's findings were very controversial. The public did not trust the conclusions, and conspiracy theories grew stronger

President Kennedy was assassinated in Dallas, Texas, on November 22, 1963. *Wikimedia Commons*

every year. Some believed that even government agencies such as the CIA and FBI could have been involved in the president's murder. Many questioned if the Warren Commission was hiding information.

In the 1970s, the US House of Representatives Select Committee on Assassinations (HSCA) began a new investigation into President Kennedy's assassination. The final report was made available in 1979. The HSCA agreed with the Warren Commission that bullets fired by Oswald, not bullets from some other firearm, had killed President Kennedy. The committee disagreed that

Crime technicians investigate a crime scene. *iStock/zoka74*

themselves and taking small particles of the scene with them when they leave.

Securing the crime area is the first step to making sure that as few people as possible come in contact with the scene in order to keep it undisturbed. Yellow crime tape is often used to block off the area, with one entrance and one exit determined. All forensic scientists who enter the crime scene must wear a cleansuit. This is a plastic suit that covers their clothing and hair. Gloves cover their hands, masks cover their noses and mouths, and plastic overshoes are worn on their feet. The scene is photographed, and written reports are made. Sometimes graphs and sketches are created as well.

A lead investigator coordinates the search and collection of evidence because each crime scene is handled differently. Is it a small area or a large one? Is it inside or outside? Answers to these questions help the lead investigator make decisions.

Oswald had definitely not conspired with anyone else. The HSCA actually concluded that there was most likely a conspiracy.

Perhaps conclusions would be more certain if the technological and scientific advances we now have had been available in 1963. There might not be as many lingering questions concerning Kennedy's death. Conspiracy theories still circulate, reflecting how many people feel unsatisfied with any investigations that have occurred.

SECURE THE SCENE

Because of Locard's Exchange Principle, today's forensic scientists understand that science begins at the crime scene. They realize that everyone coming inside the crime scene is leaving traces of

Each piece of evidence found at the scene of a crime must be collected properly before it ever enters the lab. If it is found to be tampered with or not handled according to procedures, it cannot be used as probative evidence in court. Probative evidence is evidence that is able to prove something.

Suppose soil is found on the floor of a home that has been robbed. The dirt might have been tracked in by the thief and could be traced back to the area where the criminal was prior to the robbery. Maybe it could even lead investigators to the area where the robber lives.

After the soil is photographed and documented in a report, it is removed carefully and placed in a bag. The collector must record his or her name,

Search Patterns

Searching for evidence is an important part of investigating a crime scene. Instead of randomly searching for pieces of evidence, investigators use search patterns. These methods save time and are much more effective than randomly looking around.

There are four basic search patterns:

Line: This pattern works well in large and small areas, both indoors and outdoors. For larger areas, many people might be involved. Each person starts on the same side of the area, they walk side by side across the space looking for evidence. For a small area, one person might start at one end, walking up and down the space, while the other person works from the other end, searching in the same pattern, until they meet in the middle.

Grid: This pattern is well suited for a large outside area like a field. One group walks side by side along imaginary lines going east to west. A second group works from north to south. Their paths crisscross each other. Only two people may be needed for a small area. In this case, one person starts from one side and searches north to south, back and forth. The other person searches from east to west back and forth.

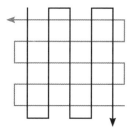

Spiral: This pattern might be best for an indoor area without a lot of furniture or a very large area. It also works well when there are few people available to help search. One person starts inside and moves in a spiral circle working further and further out until the whole area is covered. The spiral search can also start from outside and move inward. If two people are available, one can work inside out while the other one works outside in.

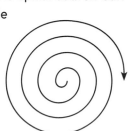

Zone: A lead investigator will section off certain areas for each person to search. When people have finished searching their area, they switch places to make sure nothing was missed.

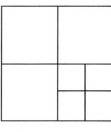

Now it's your chance to conduct a search. Have a friend "plant evidence" in a room and also in a yard, playground, or park. The evidence can be an eraser, pen, pencil, magnet, and so on, but it must be something that looks out of place in the room. Then you and two other friends must determine what search methods work best in each area, and then use them to find the evidence.

what time the evidence was collected, where it was collected, and what the evidence is. Each evidence bag has an area where this information is written.

The person who receives the bag from the collector must record his or her name, what is in the bag, where he or she was given it, and at what time. Each time the evidence changes hands, it must be documented in this way. This chain of information is called the *chain of custody*. If this chain of custody is broken, the soil evidence cannot be used in court.

SLOPPY HANDLING

In 1995, a former NFL football player named O. J. Simpson was on trial for the murder of his former wife, Nicole Brown Simpson, and her friend, Ronald Goldman. It was a highly publicized trial the whole country was talking about. All evidence seemed to indicate Simpson's guilt. During the trial, however, Simpson's lawyers constantly pointed to the mishandling of evidence by the Los Angeles police.

A thumbprint found at the scene by a detective was only photographed. It was never collected so it could be analyzed in a lab. Police did not keep the proper chain of custody with much of the evidence, either. Instead of putting each piece of evidence in separate bags, sometimes they put more than one piece in the same bag. This meant that both pieces of evidence touched and possibly contaminated each other.

The sloppy handling of blood samples threw doubt on even the strongest DNA evidence proving Simpson's guilt. Simpson was acquitted, which means that he was found not guilty and set free. It was a wake-up call to police investigators and forensic scientists everywhere.

MEOW!

It is important that investigators not overlook the smallest piece of evidence—called *trace evidence*—in their searches. Even one strand of hair could be the missing piece to help solve a crime. It could even be animal hair.

In 1994, the Royal Canadian Mounted Police discovered a jacket near the scene of a murder on Prince Edward Island. The victim was a woman named Shirley Duguay. Police suspected her

Shoe prints leave valuable clues.
iStock/eddiesimages

Tire Tread Prints

Track evidence is extremely helpful in investigations. By examining tracks, investigators can learn what types of vehicles were present at a crime scene. They may even be able to determine an exact tire that matches the print. See if you can match the tire tread to the correct tire.

You'll Need

- 4 volunteers with 4 different kinds of bikes
- washable black tempera paint and a brush
- jar of water
- 2 large white sheets of paper
- magnifying glass (optional)

1. On bike #1: Paint an even coat of washable tempera paint over part of the front tire tread. Try not to have it too watery, which will make it run, or too thick, which will make it glob. Place a sheet of white paper on the ground in front of the tire and roll the tire over the paper, making a track. (Do this on a sidewalk where you can wash off any paint that misses the paper.) Now you have created a database tire track.

2. WIthout looking, have your friends create tracks with the four bikes in different natural substances like dirt, mud, and grass.

3. Take the database tread you created and see if you can match it to the correct print. Use a magnifying glass if possible.

4. How do the different substances the track was made in affect your ability to examine the evidence? Record your observations.

Create a Shoe Print Database

A shoe print was discovered at a crime scene. The tread pattern must now be compared to shoe treads in a database to learn what kind of shoe made the print. You will make the database and your friends will see if they can find the match.

CREATE THE DATABASE

You'll Need

- copy paper
- a large dark-colored crayon with the paper around it removed
- 5 or more rubber-soled shoes with treads
- volunteers

1. Take a rubber-soled shoe with treads and place a sheet of paper over the sole.

2. Holding it in place, rub the crayon over it, long side down, until you can see the tread pattern. Try to keep the paper from moving. You have now created the first tread in your database.

3. Create rubbings of at least five different soles to complete the database.

4. Allow friends to examine one of the shoes (from a suspect). See if they can match that shoe to the correct database print.

CREATE A CAST

Sometimes shoe prints are left in material such as sand or mud. A cast must be made of the print before it changes. Take one of the shoes you used to make your database shoe print and make a cast.

You'll Need

- shoe
- hard plastic tray or foil tray with sand
- plaster of Paris
- water
- craft stick or plastic spatula
- volunteer

1. Using the "suspect's" shoe, create a cast. Take the shoe and press it into a tray filled with sand, making a distinct print indentation.

2. Mix the plaster of Paris according to the package instructions and pour it gently into the shoe print. Start at one side, pouring gently without disturbing the print, and then slowly move across the print. Pour enough to extend one to two inches (2.54–5.08 cm) around the shoe print.

3. Use a craft stick to gently smooth the top.

4. Allow the plaster to harden. This may take time—read the package instructions.

5. After the print has hardened, lift the plaster up and let it sit for a few days to make sure it is completely dry.

6. Finally, rinse the dirt off the bottom. Now you can see the details.

7. See if a friend can match it to the correct database print.

common-law husband, Douglas Beamish, who was living with his parents on the island. They believed the jacket belonged to him, but they needed more evidence.

Investigators discovered more than 20 white hairs on the jacket and decided to closely analyze them. They learned that the hairs were from a cat. Beamish's parents owned a white cat named Snowball. They needed to figure out if the fur was from Snowball.

A sample of blood was taken from Snowball and also from other cats on the island, especially those near the crime scene. The blood samples were sent to a lab in the United States, along with one of the cat hairs from the jacket. That particular hair still had the root connected, and DNA could be extracted from it. The scientists at the lab found that the DNA from the hair matched with Snowball's blood sample. This, along with other evidence, helped convict Beamish of murder and he was sentenced to prison.

EXAMINING TRACKS

Shoe prints and tire treads are extremely valuable pieces of evidence often found at crime scenes. These types of prints are collected in several ways. If a print is visible, photographs are taken, blown up to a large size, and examined.

A tire print or shoe print left on a flat surface such as concrete is often lifted using a gelatin lifter or other types of lifting film. If a print has been left in material such as sand or dirt, a cast is made of the print. Dental stone is used to create the mold.

The print mold is then taken back to the lab for analysis.

Tire treads create patterns that can be matched to specific makes of tires. The FBI has a database with thousands of tire treads. Investigators compare their found prints to those in the database to learn what brand of tire made the print. Then they can find out what type of vehicle uses that certain brand. Finally, each tire has unique characteristics from specific wear. A suspect's tire can be compared to the print by examining the specific wear areas on the tire. Perhaps there is a nick, scrape, or something similar.

Shoe prints are handled in much the same way. Sometimes investigators might contact a shoe manufacturer to learn more information about the mold that created a particular type of shoe. They might also find out what stores the shoe was distributed to.

TIRE TREAD EXPERT

Peter McDonald worked for 28 years as a tire design manager for Firestone Tire and Rubber Company in Akron, Ohio. One day, he was asked to help police in Monterey, California, analyze tire treads found at a crime scene. Tire treads had been left in the sand near two murder victims. McDonald was able to pinpoint the exact type of Firestone tires that created the tracks. He also informed police that vehicles such as dune buggies use those particular tires.

A suspect was located whose tires and car matched those described by McDonald. Then, even more evidence was found linking the suspect to the crimes, and he confessed. After that, McDonald was asked to help with other police investigations around the country.

McDonald believed that both his experience as a tire design manager and his training as an architect helped. He enjoyed creating art in many different mediums, such as painting and stained glass. He felt his artist's eye aided him in the analysis of details and patterns in his forensic work.

McDonald studied the zigzag tread patterns and raised rib areas on tire tracks. He would usually analyze them on photographs or inked impressions. He compared the tread patterns with those in his files. Once a particular tire was located, he could then begin to analyze specific unique characteristics. For instance, each tire will have specific wear areas, and maybe small cuts or marks, that can help investigators locate not just a type of tire but the exact tire.

McDonald eventually began training other police departments in the science of tire treads. In 1989, he wrote a book titled *Tire Imprint Evidence.* "I like to think of tire footprints as human fingerprints," said McDonald in a *New York Times* article in 1982. "They all have patterns that are distinguishable enough to identify and trace down."

WHERE ARE THE SHOES?

In 2013, footprints were found at the murder scene of Odin Lloyd, a semipro football player. Lloyd had been seen on video earlier in the evening with three friends. One of them was NFL football player Aaron Hernandez. Obviously, the three men were prime suspects, and inspectors believed Hernandez was the ringleader.

Detectives took photographs inside Hernandez's home during a search for evidence. They took pictures of three pairs of shoes in a closet, but they did not confiscate them. During the trial, an expert in shoe impressions concluded that the footprints at the crime scene were made by a particular type of Nike Air Jordan shoes. Hernandez's lawyers shed doubt that the shoes in the photo were the same ones that made the prints. If they had the actual shoes, though, they could easily compare the soles to the print.

When investigators went back to Hernandez's house, they found the shoes had disappeared. Because they did not collect the shoes on their first search, they missed a powerful piece of evidence they could have shared in court. In this case, there was still enough evidence brought forth during the trial for his conviction and life sentence.

NOT THE USUAL FORENSICS: FORGERIES AND CYBERCRIMES

Have you ever tried to copy someone else's handwriting? It's not as easy as it sounds. We each have a unique way of forming letters as we write. The slant of our pen and space between our letters and words are some of the very personal styles of our writing. The country or time period in which we learned to write also affects our individual handwriting.

Forensic document examiners are trained to notice the small unique qualities of the handwriting they are studying. They can determine if two pieces of handwriting are made by the same person. They can even evaluate the types of ink used to create the writing and pinpoint if a signature was traced.

A crime in 1932 proved to the American public the importance of handwriting analysis. The highly publicized case involved the infamous Charles Lindbergh, the first man to fly solo across the Atlantic Ocean. His 20-month-old son was kidnapped from his home, and a ransom note was left. Many more ransom notes followed, all demanding large sums of money. After forensic examinations, it was determined that all the ransom notes were written by the same person. Studying the letter formations, investigators also decided the writer was of German descent.

A suspect was finally located, a man named Bruno Hauptmann who was originally from Germany. Handwriting samples were collected from him and compared with the ransom notes. Eight experts all agreed it was the same handwriting.

Hauptmann was found guilty. The handwriting analysis was one very important piece of circumstantial evidence that led to his guilty verdict. Circumstantial evidence is evidence that by itself cannot definitely prove something. One piece of circumstantial evidence might not carry much weight, but when added to other evidence, it can push the scale to the side of innocence or guilt.

The Lindbergh kidnapper's ransom note.
Wikimedia Commons

ANALYZING ANCIENT WRITING USING NEW TECHNOLOGY

In 1947, some young shepherds discovered ancient manuscript scrolls near the Dead Sea in Israel. The scrolls had been preserved in large clay jars inside the Qumran caves and were named the Dead Sea Scrolls.

The manuscripts included fragments from every book in the Bible except the book of Esther, and were dated near the second century BC. This

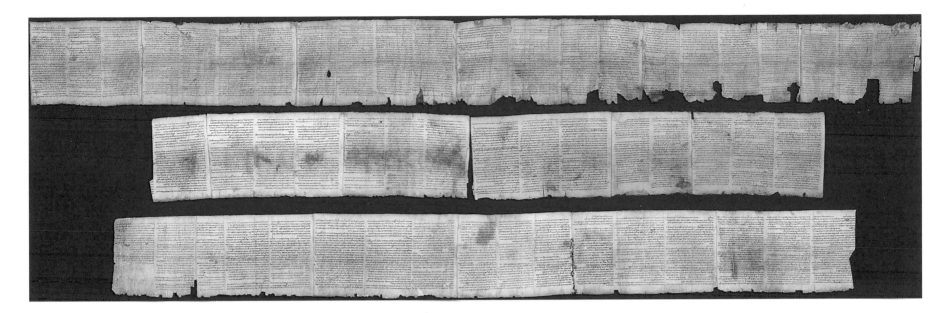

was a monumental discovery because the scrolls were the oldest manuscript of the Bible ever found. One manuscript was especially impressive. It was almost the entire book of Isaiah from the Bible written in Hebrew. This special find was called the Great Isaiah Scroll.

Manuscripts in ancient Israel were penned by trained scribes. They were professionals who learned to copy manuscripts meticulously, usually writing on animal skin or parchment. Scribes were the human copy machines in ancient days.

Through the years, as experts studied the Great Isaiah Scroll, they saw that the handwriting looked the same throughout the entire manuscript. They assumed that the same scribe had written the entire book. However, there was an empty space about halfway through the book of Isaiah that seemed to separate the two parts. Researchers wondered if this meant there might have been two different scribes who wrote each half, yet the writing looked the same to the human eye.

A team of researchers decided to use new technology to learn more about the handwriting. They programmed a computer to recognize the ink separately from the parchment background. This way, the letter shapes and different hand movements that created them could be measured and analyzed. What they found was that the two halves of the Great Isaiah Scrolls were each penned by two different scribes.

With the new discovery they had more questions. Were both scribes trained together? Were the scribes trained in such a way that they could copy another scribe's writing to finish a project? Using technology to analyze the handwriting, researchers can learn more about the writers of all the Dead Sea Scroll manuscripts and about the Jewish community that lived there.

Handwriting Analysis, Three Ways

Handwriting experts analyze the specific patterns that are unique to an individual's writing. They pay special attention to the space between letters and words. They look at how certain letters are slanted and how much pressure is applied with a writing tool.

There are many different types of analysis handwriting experts perform. Gather some friends and try these three.

- -

SIGNATURE MATCH

You'll Need

- 4 volunteers
- paper
- pens
- magnifying glass

Write a three-word sentence on a piece of paper, then write it again on another piece of paper. Have three friends each write the same sentence on a separate piece of paper. Make sure they are not trying to copy your handwriting, just to copy the sentence in their own handwriting. Be sure they use the same type of paper as well.

Give a fourth friend one of each person's handwriting samples to examine. Then give the friend one of the second samples and see if he can correctly match it to its pair. He can explain why he made the decision based on his observations.

FORGED DOCUMENT ANALYSIS

You'll Need

- 4 volunteers
- paper
- pens
- magnifying glass

Write out a four-word sentence twice, each on a separate piece of paper. Have three of your friends try their best to imitate *your* handwriting by copying your sentence on their own piece of paper. Give a fourth friend your second sample, then ask her to use magnification to see if she can determine which are forged documents and which is the original (yours).

You'll Need

- 2 volunteers
- paper
- pen

Handwriting experts can determine if a signature has been traced. They observe where a pen may have been lifted up instead of flowing naturally. They also look to see if there are shaky marks or places where the pressure changes in an unnatural way.

Have a friend or family member write his signature on a piece of paper. Trace the signature. If you need to see it better, tape the original up on a window using masking tape. Then tape your paper on top. The light from the window will help you see more clearly.

Examine the signatures using a magnifying glass. Can you tell which one is the traced signature? See if a friend or family member can tell.

DIARY DECEPTION

Falsifying documents is called *forgery*. This might involve a faked signature on a document. It also includes fake IDs, passports, birth certificates, banknotes, and, yes, even diaries.

In 1945, World War II finally ended, and Adolf Hitler, the leader of the Nazi Party, was defeated. Late in the war, a plane that supposedly carried Hitler's personal belongings had crashed. Even though the plane blew up in flames, some people believed that objects from the plane had been rescued and that someone, somewhere, had them.

In 1981, Gerd Heidemann, a reporter for *Stern*, a German magazine, told his boss some amazing news: he knew a man who had Adolf Hitler's diaries that were rescued from the crash. This was a story that could make *Stern* more famous than any other magazine in Germany, or maybe even the world.

Just to be sure the diaries were authentic, a few pages were sent to several document examiners. They all agreed that the pages were written by the same person. *Stern* magazine happily paid millions of dollars for the diaries. Heidemann made sure the payments arrived safely to his contact.

As soon as parts of the diaries were published, many historians questioned if they were real, so *Stern* editors decided to have more examinations done by forensic experts. This time, analysis revealed that the handwriting was not Hitler's at all. The types of ink and paper used did not exist before World War II, and even the bookbinding contained modern polyester material.

Upon further investigation, it was determined that a man named Konrad Kujau was the forger. Heidemann had known the diaries were fake, but he was taking part of the payments and pocketing them. Both Heidemann and Kujau were found guilty and sent to prison.

SHAKESPEARE FORGERIES

William Henry Ireland was only 17 years old when he decided to forge the writing of one of the most famous playwrights and poets of all time. Samuel Ireland, William Henry's father, was an enthusiastic admirer of William Shakespeare, and an avid collector of antique items. Eager to receive his father's positive attention in some way, William Henry chose to create what his father wanted most in his collection: Shakespeare's handwriting.

In 1794, William Henry found a picture in a book of a signature and mortgage deed written by Shakespeare. He then copied it. He used diluted ink to make the writing look faded and wrote on aged parchment paper. Then he added waxed seals he found on an old document in the law office where he worked.

William Henry told his father that he had found the writing in a collection of documents that a wealthy acquaintance had given him. He said the man had no interest in the old papers and gave them to William Henry to deal with. When Samuel saw the document, he immediately believed it was authentic and encouraged his son to search for more.

As William Henry created more forged Shakespeare letters, poems, and plays, his father enthusiastically shared them with his literary friends. They too accepted them as authentic without any investigation. They were particularly curious about two plays they had never heard of before, which of course were created by William Henry, not Shakespeare.

In 1776, the owner of Drury Lane Theatre in London decided to premiere one of the newly discovered Shakespeare plays called *Vortigern*. But about the same time, much suspicion about the "Shakespeare writings" began circulating. When those attending the play laughed at it, William Henry decided to finally confess.

William Henry's father never accepted the fact that the writings were forged by his son. For him, what he wanted to believe overpowered the actual facts. Handwriting analysis would have put such fraud to rest before it grew out of control had someone gone to the trouble to ask for it from the start.

FROM FORGERY TO FBI

Fraud is a word used to describe criminal methods of obtaining money. Forging checks is a type of fraud. Before debit cards were widely used, people typically wrote checks or used cash to pay for things. Criminals would steal checks or create them and then forge the owner's signature on the check. It took time for the check to process. The check owner might not realize for several weeks that money was removed from his or her account

Chromatography

Chromatography is the process used for separating the different components that make up a substance. In handwriting analysis, forensic scientists use chromatography to learn what kind of ink was used on a document. This might help them understand what type of writing tool was used or if it was an old or more modern type of ink. It could even link a suspect to a forged document.

You'll Need

- 5 coffee filters cut in half or a sheet of paper towel cut into one-inch (2.54 cm) strips
- black ink pen
- 3 different brands of washable black markers
- washable black dry erase board marker
- 1 or more jars of water
- volunteer

1. Sign your name on one of the paper towels or coffee filter strips using the first washable marker. Make sure your friend does not see which brand of marker you use.

2. Allow your friend to dip your signed paper into the jar of water just below the signature, as shown. Do not dip the signature in the water. Fold the top of the paper over the side of the jar and wait for the water to soak up through the paper and ink.

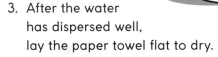

3. After the water has dispersed well, lay the paper towel flat to dry.

4. Now have your friend test the different markers and paper strips to determine which one was used on the signature. She will draw a thick line across the bottom of each strip about an inch (2.54 cm) from the bottom. Mark the top of the paper with the name of the pen she used.

5. One at a time, dip the paper into the water just below the ink line and fold the top of the paper over the edge of the jar. Allow the water to disperse. Then lay it flat and observe the results.

6. After the samples have dried, have your friend examine each pen sample. In the experiment, which ink reacted the same as the signature ink? See if your friend can choose the correct pen.

to pay for things he or she did not buy. Criminals also created fake checks and fake IDs of accounts and people that didn't exist. They could then write many checks—until they were caught, of course.

Frank Abagnale is a man well known for his forgery crimes and for his FBI service. In 1964, when he was only 16, Abagnale began a forging spree that spread across the world. It began when he ran away from home after a court judge shared

Bessie Blount Griffin: Forensic Handwriting Expert

Bessie Blount was born in 1914 in Hickory, Virginia, and attended a small segregated elementary school there. Her teacher scolded her and struck her on the hand when she saw Bessie using her left hand to write. Back in those days, teachers believed you must write only with your right hand, a difficult task for those born left-handed. Bessie decided she would learn to write not only with her right hand but with her toes and teeth as well.

There were no African American schools in her area for grades above six. After she and her family moved to New Jersey, Bessie studied on her own and earned her GED. A GED is equivalent to a high school diploma. She then continued her education, earning a nursing degree, and became a registered physical therapist.

Blount began working in hospitals with many World War II veterans. Some of them were amputees, having lost limbs in the war. Blount taught those with no arms how to hold utensils using their toes and teeth. She also invented a device that patients could use to feed themselves. When a patient bit on a tube, it engaged a motor that delivered a bite of food through a mouthpiece. Blount created many other inventions to help people with disabilities.

During their recovery, Blount also helped patients with their writing. She saw that each patient's handwriting had unique qualities and patterns. She also observed how their physical improvements affected their handwriting. She published a paper titled "Medical Graphology" in 1968 about her observations.

Blount's interest in handwriting led her to become a certified handwriting expert, and she served several police departments. By 1972, she had become the chief examiner for the Portsmouth, Virginia, police department. Then, in 1977, she attended training at the prestigious Scotland Yard in its Document Division.

Finally, Blount started her own business. She worked as a handwriting expert determining the authenticity of documents. Sometimes her clients were police departments, but other times they were museums or collectors. Many of the documents she examined involved the slave trade, Civil War papers, and US Native American treaties. She continued running her business until she was 85.

the sudden and traumatic news that his parents were getting a divorce and he must choose which one to live with.

Abagnale altered his driver's license to change his age to 26. The older age helped him get better jobs and earn more money. Then, when he realized he still did not make enough to support himself, he began writing checks from his empty bank account. To avoid getting caught, he decided to move from his home state of New York. He realized, though, that his out-of-town checks might not be accepted anymore. That is when he began impersonating an airline pilot. He reasoned that pilots were respected and trusted individuals.

After obtaining a pilot's uniform and creating a fake pilot's ID, he was allowed to travel for free on flights. This was a perk all pilots enjoyed when they wanted a vacation. With his new ID and uniform, he could cash checks and pay for goods all over the world without any questions.

Abagnale quickly ended up on many wanted lists, including the FBI's. Eventually, he was apprehended in France in 1969 when a flight attendant who was a former girlfriend saw him buying groceries and turned him in. He served six months in a French prison cell with no electricity or plumbing or even a bed. When he entered prison, he weighed 198 pounds. He left weighing only 109. He then served another six months in a Swedish prison before he was transferred to the United States.

After he served four years of his 12-year sentence in a US prison, the federal government made him an offer: if he would help authorities apprehend criminals like himself for the remaining eight years of his sentence, he would be set free. He agreed. Abagnale ended up working with the FBI for more than 40 years investigating crimes such as fraud, identity theft, and cybercrime.

COPYCAT

Documents, banknotes, and IDs are not the only things faked. Copying famous art has been around for a long time. For centuries art students have copied famous artwork in order to grow in their own skills. This is not a problem. But it becomes a crime when someone copies a piece of art and then sells it as though it were the original. Also, a person who creates a piece of artwork and signs it with someone else's signature, and then sells it, has committed forgery.

Some artwork sells for millions of dollars. Usually, this is artwork created by people who lived long ago, like Rembrandt or Van Gogh. Because the paintings are so old, it is often impossible to track where they originally came from. Collectors, museums, and art galleries are always on the lookout for special pieces to buy.

MASTERPIECE OR MISTAKE?

The Metropolitan Museum of Art in New York is well known for its collection of famous artwork. In the early 1920s, the museum purchased three statues of Etruscan warriors. The ancient statues were a rare find. The museum paid tens of thousands of dollars for them. That amount of money would be equal to millions of dollars today.

Forging Artwork

Give your friends a chance to see how well they can forge a "masterpiece" you've painted.

- - - - - - - - - - - - - -

You'll Need

- tempera or acrylic paint
- paintbrushes
- water
- painting canvases
- 2 volunteers

1. Paint a landscape of your own. Add some trees and maybe some water, but keep it simple.

2. Have two friends try and copy your painting.

3. Examine the three paintings. Which one looks most like yours? What details are missing? What about brushstrokes and thickness of paints?

4. Discuss the differences with your friends.

In 1933, the statues were proudly displayed as one of the museum's prized possessions. Italian art historians expressed concern about the authenticity of the statues from time to time, but no one was concerned enough to investigate further. The statues were black, just as Etruscan statues should be. There were cracks on the surface, and one had an arm and finger missing. Surely these were clear signs of aging. Or were they?

Finally, in 1960, after the statues had been on display for 28 years, forensic testing was conducted on their black glaze. Chemical tests revealed that the glaze contained ingredients that ancient Italian sculptors did not use. This proved that the statues were fakes.

Soon after that, a man named Alfredo Fioravanti admitted that he and his friend Riccardo Riccardi had created the fake statues. Fioravanti still had the finger broken off one of the warriors to prove it. Riccardi had already died by then, but Fioravanti went to jail.

I PROMISE, IT'S REAL

Works of art created today are sold with a paper called a *certificate of authenticity*. Much like your birth certificate proves who you are, the authenticity document proves who the artwork is by. Other documents may accompany a piece of artwork, serving as a type of chain of custody. Each document shows who bought the artwork, the date, and who the piece was purchased from. As you have learned, though, even these documents

Art Forgery Confession

Han van Meegeren was born in the Netherlands in 1889. Van Meegeren had a natural artistic talent that led him to study art. He became an art teacher and eventually a professional painter. Opinions from art critics were extremely important to a painter's art career. The art "experts" criticized Van Meegeren's work. They felt it was not original enough.

Van Meegeren wanted to get back at the art critics and prove that they were not the experts they claimed to be. He decided to create forgeries that would fool them. He chose a famous Dutch old master artist named Jan Vermeer. There are not many records of Vermeer's life and only 36 known paintings by him. Van Meegeren knew art dealers would relish the idea of finding a rare Vermeer painting to have in their collection.

Van Meegeren spent years trying to perfect his forgery technique. He mixed a synthetic plastic with his paints; this kept them from dissolving when tested with alcohol. The plastic would also make it seem as though the paints were like the authentic old paints that Vermeer used. He heated the paintings in an oven, hardening them. Then, he rolled the canvas up, creating cracks to make the painting appear older. He even pushed some dirt inside the cracks. He sold many "Vermeer paintings" this way, fooling the experts and making millions of dollars.

After World War II, Van Meegeren sold one of his forged Vermeers to an art dealer who, in turn, did business with high-ranking Nazi officials. Instead of selling the "Vermeer" to them, the art dealer traded the painting for 137 stolen paintings. Nazis had stolen many European paintings during the war and hidden them in various places. Van Meegeren, though, was accused of selling a prized Vermeer to the enemy. Such a charge was a very serious one. He was brought to trial in 1945 and faced the dilemma of being accused as a traitor or confessing to forgery. He decided to confess.

At first, officials did not believe him. He had to paint a "Vermeer" while being watched to prove he could forge a Vermeer painting. Suddenly, he became somewhat of a hero. He had fooled the Nazis with his fake painting, causing them to hand over 137 stolen paintings. His sentence became a light one, only one year in prison. However, he died of a heart attack before serving it.

Han van Meegeren in his studio. *Wikimedia Commons*

Security features on a modern $100 bill.
iStock/Diy13

US money is printed by the Bureau of Engraving and Printing. The banknotes, or bills, must be created in such a way that they cannot be produced by counterfeiters. Creating fake money is nothing new. As with everything else, though, technology has created new challenges in fighting counterfeit crime. Access to scanners and inkjet printers has given crooks easier methods to create fake money. In response, new technology must be employed in the designs of new bills.

Newer bills have many security features, making them extremely hard to reproduce. For example, now bills contain tiny fine threads of ink that cannot be reproduced by scanners and printers. They have watermarks embedded when the bills are made and special inks that change colors when the bills are held at different angles. The watermark on the $10 bill is a portrait of Alexander Hamilton. When the bill is held under a light, his invisible face becomes visible. On the same bill, a tiny thread of ink turns orange under UV light.

To learn more about US currency and see the security features of each bill, visit www.uscurrency.gov.

HIGH-TECH HEIST

Today's forensic scientists tackle crimes that even Sherlock Holmes never imagined. As new technologies constantly develop, so do new types of crimes. In the past, thieves went to a bank building to rob it. Now, they can sit at a computer, break into someone's bank account, and steal money without leaving their own house. Stealing

can be forged. Art dealers estimate that half of the art being sold today is fake.

The types of paints and other materials artists used in the past are completely different from those used today. Forensic experts can examine the materials of a piece of art using fluorescent lights and x-rays. They can carefully test small areas of a painting with chemicals. Cracks in older paintings are called *craquelure*. Experts understand how these crack patterns are supposed to look if they are authentic. They can use magnification to study the craquelure and if it is real or simply created to look old.

COUNTERFEIT MONEY

Maybe you have heard the expression "Money doesn't grow on trees." Have you ever wondered where money really *does* come from?

personal information such as a social security number or credit card number is often done with the click of a computer mouse.

In the 1980s, home computers became commonplace for the first time. As with all new types of forensics, it took a while for guidelines to develop for digital forensics. A serious cybercrime in 1986 caused forensic investigators to create standards in this new field. That is when a computer programmer named Cliff Stoll made a startling discovery.

Stoll started working for a national scientific research lab in California. On his first day of work, he was looking into a small math error using one of the computers. He discovered someone was hacking into the company's computer system. Gaining access to someone's computer without permission is called *hacking*.

Eventually, FBI agents joined Stoll and they tracked down the intruder, a man from Germany named Markus Hess. Hess and his friends were hacking into computers that contained important information. They were actually stealing military and nuclear secrets from the United States and other countries. Then they were selling the information to Soviet Russia. Hess and his friends were convicted of espionage (spying).

Stealing information is just one type of crime that digital forensic scientists handle. Computers, phones, and other technical devices often provide information that helps forensic scientists in their investigations of other crimes.

For instance, if a computer is found at a suspect's home, it might contain valuable information that could help solve a crime. Perhaps an e-mail, text, or Internet site that was searched might link a suspect to a crime. Forensic investigators follow set procedures to examine a computer, just as they do with all evidence. They must photograph every step of their investigation. The computer hard drive is especially valuable because of all the stored information it contains.

WHEN COMPUTERS GET SICK

People are not the only ones that are susceptible to viruses. Computers are too. A computer virus is a program that someone has designed for the purpose of infecting other computer systems.

Computer virus detected.
IStock/Rawf8

Tony Fullman: Cybersecurity Engineer

Tony Fullman works as a senior cybersecurity engineer for the military. When asked to describe her work, she says, "I find bad guys in computers." Cybercrime is when criminals gain access to the information on computers and either steal it, damage it, or both.

Any type of video site such as YouTube, TikTok, and video game sites can potentially invite bad guys into your computer. Fullman describes several ways criminals do this. Often sites such as YouTube will have a link pop up under the video being viewed. When the link is clicked, it is like opening a locked door and allowing a bad guy in.

"Think of your computer as your house," says Tony. "You have the doors and windows locked. When you click on a bad link, it is like you have unlocked your door, inviting thieves inside. Now they freely move around, stealing credit card numbers, phone numbers, and files. They quickly use the credit cards to buy lots of stuff on Amazon and rack up your parents' credit card bill."

Another common way a cybercriminal sneaks into computers is through websites. Perhaps you are browsing a website in order to research a school project. You see one site that looks like it might contain a lot of great information. When

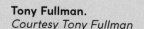

Tony Fullman.
Courtesy Tony Fullman

you click on it, you notice many ads popping up. These pop-ups are called "potentially unwanted applications." Sometimes, these pop-ups are downloading applications in your computer that unlock the door to intruders. "Be careful," warns Fullman, "when using websites, games, and movie sites. Don't trust the ads you see pop up. Before you click on a link to a website, make sure it is the actual website address of the place you are trying to visit and not a site that is trying to look like the real one."

If you want to become a cybersecurity analyst, Fullman suggests four years of college studying information systems, then a master's degree in cybersecurity. Most companies have their own cybersecurity teams. They are paid to constantly look for intruders inside their companies' computers and keep information secure. But what if they find someone who has broken into their system? "That is when the forensics team comes in," says Fullman.

Forensic computer scientists hook up their own computer to a computer they are investigating. They learn what e-mails, websites, and files are on the computer. When they scan the computer hard drive, examiners can even see any deleted e-mails and websites that were visited.

Criminals may think they have deleted information so no one can find it. Anything deleted is still on the hard drive of a computer, and forensic investigators can find it all. A SIM card on a phone is like a hard drive on a computer. Forensic experts use a cellular exploiting device that grabs all the information from the phone. Then the information is scanned and printed on a spreadsheet for the forensic team to study.

Fullman has many stories, but one in particular stands out. She was working for a company as a cybersecurity analyst when she recognized a name that popped up from her military experience. The name belonged to a bad guy in another country. She saw that a client of the company she was working for was doing business with him. Extremely large amounts of money were going from the client to this man. No one else would have recognized the name other than Tony. There is no telling how long the "business" transactions would have continued if she had not been there to catch this name.

Tony has a bachelor's degree in computer science and biological science. She also earned a master's degree in biological, political, and computer sciences and a PhD in cybersecurity.

Sometimes the virus might just create a simple annoyance. Other times, it can destroy important information.

Usually viruses enter a computer one of two ways. One way is through an e-mail. When the recipient clicks on a link sent by a legitimate-looking e-mail, a virus is automatically installed. The other way is through fake sites that a person may click on while searching the Internet. When the site is clicked, the virus steps in. Computer antivirus software is installed on computers to try and block viruses from entering.

THE LOVE BUG VIRUS

In May 2000, computers around the world received e-mails titled "I Love You" that resembled Valentine's Day messages. When recipients clicked on the attached document, a virus entered their computer system. Then it sent the same e-mail to every contact in the victim's computer address book. This infected millions of computers. Many companies and government agencies' e-mail systems crashed under the overload.

At that time, most people did not have virus-protecting software on their computers like we do today. People usually did not bother to back up their work either. The damage was extensive, costing billions of dollars. Investigators studied the virus code and tracked the intrusion to the Philippines. A 23-year-old student there named Onel de Guzman had created the virus as part of a school project. At that time, the Philippines had no laws against computer hacking. This meant that de Guzman was never brought to justice for the havoc and loss he inflicted on others.

The Great Worm Infects Computers

On November 2, 1988, a graduate student from Cornell University intended to create a prank involving a few computers at various locations. The "prank" quickly sped out of control, infecting thousands of computers and resulting in millions of dollars in damages.

Twenty-three-year-old Robert Morris created a type of computer infection called a *worm*. Unlike a virus, a worm does not need someone to click on a link or fake e-mail to allow it to spread. A worm can infiltrate a computer system and slither from computer to computer without anyone accidentally opening a door to it.

Among the many computers the Morris worm infected were ones at Princeton and Stanford Universities and NASA. Morris claimed he never intended for so many computers to be infected. He tried to send an anonymous apology with instructions on how to remove the worm, but it was too late—the damage was done.

A jury found Morris guilty of breaking federal law. Just a few years prior, in 1986, the Computer Fraud and Abuse Act had been enacted. Morris was the first person ever convicted under this new law. He was fined, put on probation, and given 400 hours of community service.

The Morris worm woke the public up from a false sleep of cybersafety. It inspired the creation of security systems to protect computers from viruses and worms. Today, programmers are constantly working to create software that blocks malicious worms like this one.

TERRORISM TECHNOLOGY

New viruses are always being developed by criminals. There are even viruses that steal all the files on someone else's computer while the thief holds them for ransom. Unless the victim pays the amount asked for, the files are not returned. Sometimes, even if the ransom is paid, the files are never returned. Computer programmers are kept busy developing new antivirus software to protect people's computers. Forensic scientists are always working to develop new ways of catching these cyberthieves.

A particularly malicious ransomware attacks hospitals, schools, and university computers. With this type of attack, a whole organization is left without the important information it needs. Many businesses cannot afford expensive protective software to keep their computers safe, so they are left vulnerable to attacks. The ransom software is also becoming much more sophisticated and harder to combat. Even police departments and city governments have been hit by this terrorist technology.

In 2019, the city of Baltimore, Maryland, was attacked with a ransomware virus. The city government's e-mail and phone systems were shut down and important information locked up. The online billing services of many city services, including electricity, were taken down as well. The hacker demanded $80,000. The attack left the city in a horrible situation, but the Baltimore mayor refused to pay. It took months for the city to recover from the damage, which cost over $18 million.

Cybersecurity specialists warn victims to never pay ransoms. No one knows who the money is going to or what criminal or terrorist activity it may be funding. Also, the hacker may put something in the returned system to harm it again later. There is no guarantee that the system will even be returned at all.

In some cases, officials choose to pay a ransom because the stolen information is so vital; it might be far cheaper and faster to pay a ransom than to update an entire computer network that was broken into.

In May 2021, one of the largest pipelines in the US was forced to shut down because the computer network that operates it had been hacked. The Colonial Pipeline supplies millions of barrels of fuel to certain areas in the US. The shutdown created a huge shortage. People needed gasoline to travel to work. Truckers needed fuel to transport their goods. Colonial Pipeline administrators reluctantly paid a ransom of $4.4 million to get things moving again.

Computers and digital devices make life easier and more efficient in many ways. This is why, in many elections, voting machines have taken the place of counting ballots by hand. They save time. But can these voting machines be hacked? Andrew Appel, a professor of computer science at Princeton University believes they can. He and his colleagues have easily hacked into numerous voting machines through the years simply to prove his point.

Appel suggests voters use hand marked paper ballots that are counted by an optical-scan machine. If the scanners are somehow hacked, the machine counts can be compared with the physical ballots to discover any differences. He also suggests routinely checking the paper votes against the scanning machine numbers.

While voting machines have improved over the years, many people feel they will always be vulnerable to hacks. This is an important issue in every election. Voters want to be certain that elected officials are chosen by the majority of voters and not by hackers.

FORENSIC ACCOUNTING

Forensic accountants are specialists who are trained to find cheating in financial records. They work for individual companies to keep an eye on the accounting to make sure all is computed correctly and honestly. They also work for investigation firms, which hire them to search financial records of organizations that are under investigations.

Enron, located in Houston, Texas, was one of the largest energy companies in the world in the early 1990s. Many business professionals invested their money in Enron's stocks. They wanted to be

Hacking into the Cookie

See how quickly your friends can hack into your locked information and grab the cookie.

You'll Need

- cookie
- combination bike lock
- volunteer
- paper and pen

1. Hide a cookie where it is out of sight. Then set a combination on a bike lock that is easy for you to remember. Your number choices must be based on personal information, such as the date you were born, your phone number, address, favorite numbers, etc.

2. Write out a code on a piece of paper. The code must contain 3-7 rows of no more than 10 letters each. Each row of letters must contain letters when put together create one word. All the words from each row should form a sentence or phrase that gives directions to the location of the hidden cookie.

3. Have a friend see if he can figure out the bike lock's combination by asking you questions: your birthday, favorite numbers, etc. When and if he figures it out and opens it, hand him the code you created. See if he can unscramble the words and decipher the directions. Your friend has five minutes to figure it out and get the cookie or it's yours. If you want, try the activity again, with the roles reversed!

part of the booming company's success. Enron's growing business required thousands of employees to function efficiently. Many of the employees also invested in the company's stock.

At some point, things changed for Enron. The company began to experience huge losses, yet none of the investors were aware of it. Neither were the employees. That is because top officials in the company did not report the huge losses. They lied to clients and employees, hiding the facts. On top of that, officials were making money from their lies while clients were losing money.

Enron officials were able to hide their criminal dealings by creating false accounting methods and financial reporting. In 2001, the company filed for bankruptcy. Bankruptcy is an action taken by companies when they have too much debt to repay. People wondered how this could happen to Enron. Weren't they doing well according to their financial records and reports? The bankruptcy raised concerns that something was not right.

In 2002, FBI agents and other investigators began searching through the company's corporate headquarters to find out what was going on. Forensic accountants and computer analysts searched through Enron's massive amounts of computer data. Investigators tracked bank accounts and looked at financial records. They found that Enron officials had committed fraud, basically stealing money from their clients and employees. Investors lost millions of dollars. Employees lost their jobs and retirement savings.

In the end, 22 people were convicted of crimes relating to Enron's fraud, including the president of the company. As a result of the Enron scandal, President George W. Bush signed the Sarbanes-Oxley Act in 2002. This legislation established new regulations for public companies. Companies now must adhere to much stricter accounting practices and financial reporting.

FORENSIC ACCOUNTING
CATCHES CAPONE

Sometimes, forensic accountants are the ones who help put violent criminals in jail when other legal methods don't work. For instance, Al Capone, the head of Chicago's "Mob," committed heinous crimes in the 1920s. He paid others to do his dirty work, including murders. He silenced those who did not comply with his wishes. Often, he used bribes and threats to avoid arrest. He was apprehended and jailed, but only for short periods. There was never enough evidence to keep him for long and get him off the streets.

Finally, in 1931, after a two-year investigation, things changed. Investigator and accountant Frank Wilson gathered enough evidence to prove

Enron Headquarters.
Flickr/Alex

Capone was guilty of fraud. Capone had not disclosed his correct income to the government for tax payment, as he was legally required to do. Most of Capone's income came from criminal practices. He certainly was not going to honestly disclose that to the government. As a result, he broke the law by not paying the correct taxes. Capone was sentenced to 11 years in prison and large court fines. When he got out, he was too sickly to continue his life of crime.

6 FIRES AND EXPLOSIONS

What if most or all of the evidence in a crime scene has been destroyed by fire? This adds a whole new set of challenges for forensic investigators. The deliberate burning of a home, business, or personal property is called *arson*, and there are several reasons someone might commit this crime. A fire might help cover up evidence of a robbery or murder by destroying fingerprints and trace evidence. Sometimes a fire is started by the owner of a home or business in order to collect insurance money.

Forensic fire investigators are trained to discover and test the remains left after a fire. Through observation and testing, they can learn how a fire started. Perhaps it was not arson. Maybe it was an act of nature, such as lightning, or an accident, like a candle left burning. It could have been caused by faulty wiring or a gas explosion. Forensic fire experts use scientific methods to solve fire mysteries. What they learn can not only solve crimes but also help engineers build safer structures.

DON'T STAND TOO CLOSE TO THE FIRE

In the 1700s, you wouldn't want to stand too close to a burning home. If you did, that might be all that was needed to accuse you of starting the fire. Destroying someone's home or property was not taken lightly. Fires spread quickly in the typical wooden structures of the day, and could literally destroy a whole city. Arson was a serious crime, so serious that in England you could be sentenced to death if found guilty. (In 1860 the punishment was reduced to merely life in prison.)

In the early 20th century, investigators had their hands full trying to solve all the robberies and murders in crowded cities. Arson fell to the side, and the laws became less strict. And besides, there were not a lot of scientific methods to determine how fires started. Investigators depended on their observation skills more than anything—they learned to look for fire patterns.

Fire patterns are visual charred remains left on walls and floors from a fire. Investigators learned to examine these patterns in order to understand how the fire moved through the structure. This helped them determine what started it and where it started. For example, usually fires create a V pattern as they move up and out from the starting point. Often fire patterns were used as evidence to prove arson. But what if the patterns were misunderstood?

THE SCIENCE OF FLASHOVER

In 1990, John Lentini, a forensic arson expert, was asked to examine fire debris in a suspected arson case. A man named Gerald Lewis was suspected of starting a fire in his home that killed his family. Lentini had been told that debris from the fire contained gasoline. This would help prove that Gerald Lewis had used gasoline to intentionally ignite a fire. Yet when Lentini conducted a chemical analysis on the debris, he found no traces of gasoline. More evidence of arson was needed to take the case to trial.

Lentini decided he needed to set up a fire test in a house down the street from the Lewis home. It was going to be torn down soon, and it had the same floor plan as the Lewis home. Firefighters brought in furnishings that exactly matched those of the Lewis house. Then they set fire to the sofa, imitating how the Lewis house fire had started. They set video cameras up to record what happened. What they learned changed everything.

Linking Evidence to a Suspect

Finding evidence that links a suspect to a crime can be like finding a needle in a haystack. Investigators must search very carefully and discern what is evidence and what is not. See how you and your friends do collecting evidence left at a crime scene, where a thief has broken into a room and stolen money from a box.

You'll Need

- 4 or more volunteers
- several personal items from one volunteer such as a pen, notebook, sock, or hairpin
- magnifying glass

1. Select one of your friends to be the "investigator." Have that person leave the room.

2. Ask the remaining friends to choose who will be the "thief."

3. Plant seven pieces of "evidence" in the room that represent that particular person (thief). Ideas include a strand of hair, personal items such as a pen, notebook, sock, hairpin, etc. Plant some of the evidence in difficult locations to find, such as under a couch or between two cushions.

4. Optional: you might add a dirty shoe print or a fingerprint on a glass.

5. Ask the "investigator" to return to the room. Tell the investigator that money was stolen from a box in the room, but don't give any additional information.

6. Now, allow the "investigator" to search for and collect the evidence and see if she can determine who the thief is. Make sure she has a magnifying glass.

ATF Fire Research Lab

The largest indoor forensic fire lab in the world is The ATF's fire research lab in Beltsville, Maryland. Built in 2002, the huge facility contains many kinds of lab rooms. One room is a whopping 16,900 square feet (1,570 sq. m), where a two-story building can be constructed for large-scale fire tests. Smaller fire rooms can accommodate testing the effects of fire on specific types of materials.

A multiscreen video system helps with recording and analyzing fire research. Thermal imaging cameras allow scientists to see through smoke and record temperatures within different areas of the fire they are testing. Inside the controlled setting, special hoods and exhaust systems keep fire fumes from polluting the environment.

Some of the research that is conducted at the lab incudes fire patterns, materials that ignite fires, and flashovers. Fire scientists, engineers, and investigators can recreate fire scenes to test different hypotheses. Evidence from fire scenes is also examined at the lab. In addition, fire investigators are trained there.

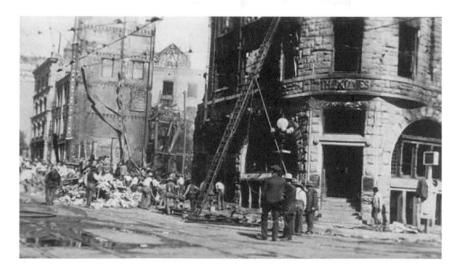

The bombed rubble of the *Los Angeles Times* building, 1910. *Wikimedia Commons*

As they observed the test fire, they saw that the flashover occurred much sooner than expected. Flashover is when a fire becomes so hot that everything around it suddenly ignites in an explosion of flames. This understanding backed up Gerald Lewis's story of what had occurred. There was not enough evidence now to bring the case to trial.

Lentini began studying flashovers more extensively and training other people. He knew that patterns can easily be misread by investigators if they do not have a clear understanding of how flashovers occur. Now, as new technologies are always developing, fire forensics is much more of an accurate science than it used to be.

BOOM!

A forensic arson scientist works closely with forensic explosives experts. Together they try to learn what has caused an explosion. Was it an accident or criminal act? These are the questions forensic investigators try to answer as they look for evidence to examine and test.

Through the years, there have been many explosions in factories and mills, especially before building code standards were written. Most often, the explosions resulted from poorly constructed buildings and poor safety habits, not criminal activity. However, in the early 1900s, a series of dynamite bombs were set off in various cities in the United States. Anarchist groups that disagreed with government decisions and policies were behind the deadly crimes.

In one of the explosions, the *Los Angeles Times* building was destroyed and 21 workers were killed. The *Los Angeles Times* was a newspaper that apparently published stories that someone didn't like. Two brothers, James and John McNamara, were held accountable. They were found by keen detective work.

BOMB SNIFFERS

Today's bomb experts follow standard procedures and use sophisticated tools. Sometimes they are trying to find an explosive device and other times they are dealing with a known bomb.

When searching for explosives, bomb experts sometimes use bomb-sniffing dogs. A dog's sense of smell is approximately 40 times more sensitive than a human's. The dogs are trained to smell explosive chemicals and alert their human partners, called *handlers*. You may have seen these dogs in airports, where they are used to sniff suspicious bags.

Before 1972, you would not have seen a bomb-sniffing dog in an airport. An event that year made everyone aware of how valuable these specially trained animals are. A Trans World Airlines (TWA) plane was on its way to Los Angeles from John F. Kennedy International Airport (JFK) in New York. The pilot of Flight 7 received a call just 15 minutes after takeoff with news that a bomb might be on board the plane. The pilot turned the plane around and landed back at JFK, where the passengers were quickly taken off the plane to safety.

Puppies Behind Bars: Training Bomb-Sniffing Dogs

While there are many schools that train bomb-sniffing dogs around the country, there is one that is quite unusual. At Puppies Behind Bars, training dogs actually begins in prison. For the first year of their lives, puppies are trained by selected prison inmates. The program allows prisoners to help society and have a sense of purpose. At the same time, the trainers get a lot of love and affection from the puppies. Labrador retrievers are among the most common breed they train. These dogs desire to please and are highly motivated by rewards such as food, toys, and praise.

Many of the dogs that graduate from Puppies Behind Bars go on to further training at other facilities for specific bomb-sniffing duties. These dogs are used to sniff out explosive chemicals in banks, airports, offices, and public gatherings, to name a few. Some even go on to serve in the government and military.

Puppies Behind Bars is located in New York and began in 1997. It started as a school for training guide dogs for the blind. Now, it also trains dogs to help first responders and recovering war veterans. After the 9/11 terrorist attacks, Puppies Behind Bars began training bomb-sniffing dogs to meet the increasing need for this type of service dog.

Training a bomb-sniffing dog.
Wikimedia Commons

Bomb-Sniffing Bugs

Washington University in St. Louis is in the process of developing ways to use locusts to locate explosives. Locusts can determine a difference in smells within milliseconds. Scientists are learning how they can use this ability to help with bomb detection.

Electrons are surgically placed in the bug's brain. These devices gather information about what the bug is smelling. The bugs are then instructed which way to fly by a small type of stamp made of silk placed on their wings. A laser light can heat up the wing, causing the bug to fly in a desired direction. Once the bug has reached its target, embedded sensors cause its antennae to glow different colors, alerting the bug's handler if the locust is smelling an explosive chemical.

Flight 7 was not the only one grounded. All TWA flights were ordered to land. An anonymous caller had told airline authorities that bombs were aboard several planes and unless $2 million were handed over, the bombs would explode.

By coincidence, there was a group of bomb-sniffing dogs in a demonstration at JFK. Brandy, a German shepherd, was taken to Flight 7, where she quickly found a briefcase labeled CREW in the cockpit. After she sniffed it, she sat down by it, alerting her handler. Brandy had found the explosive device. It was immediately taken away and unarmed just five minutes before it was set to explode. Fortunately, no other explosives were found on any other flights.

In 1973, President Richard Nixon helped to create the TSA's Explosives Detection Canine Team Program. After starting with just 40 teams in 20 airports, the program now has canine teams in airports all across the United States. In addition, bomb-sniffing dogs are often used for security at sports events and other venues where large amounts of people gather.

WE FOUND IT!

Disarming a bomb is a dangerous mission. Robots are often used for this job instead of people. Much like a drone, an operator controls the robot from afar, staying out of harm's way. Cameras are attached to the robot so that the controller can see what the robot sees. Robots can be very small, while others are the size of a small- or medium-sized vehicle. Some contain arms that allow different tools to be attached to them. These types of robots have been used for many years and continue to grow more sophisticated as technology advances.

When forensic bomb specialists are investigating a bomb that has already exploded, they are searching for evidence such as wires, switches, bomb fragments, and bomb residue. All the evidence is carefully sealed in containers and studied in the lab. A type of switch or wire might be traced back to a specific shop where it was purchased and lead investigators one step closer to a suspect who ignited the bomb. They are also hoping some of the gathered evidence might contain fingerprints or DNA. In addition, chemical analyses of bomb residue can help them learn what type of bomb was used.

CRASH!

In the 1900s, forensic science focused on individual crimes like theft and murder. It was not ready for the large-scale crime that occurred in 1933 when a US airplane blew up in midair over Chesterton, Indiana, from an explosive device on board. Seven people were killed. It was the first time a US passenger plane had been attacked this way.

The investigation by FBI agents led only to the understanding that it was in fact an explosive device that caused the crash. No answers about its origin were ever found. The forensic tools and training that were needed were simply not available for an explosion of this magnitude.

In 1955, when another airplane crash occurred, FBI forensic examiners were ready to solve the mystery that caused it. United Airlines Flight 629 was heading to Portland, Oregon, from Denver, Colorado. It crashed in the countryside along the way, killing 44 people on board. One hundred FBI investigators joined a team of airline specialists to find and collect the airplane debris that was scattered for miles around the crash site.

They drew a grid to represent the area and carefully recorded where each fragment was found. Pieces were sent to a large warehouse in Colorado where the airplane was reassembled as much as possible. They discovered that a large hole had been made by a huge blast where luggage was stored. This was not the place where a mechanical problem would normally occur. They believed it must have been a bomb.

Five very small pieces covered with an unusual soot were also found. When forensic examiners studied the pieces in the lab, they found dynamite residue. Leather fragments from one piece of luggage revealed it was damaged more than the others. The luggage was traced to a wealthy woman named Daisie King.

Pieces of United Airlines Flight 629 reconstructed.
Wikimedia Commons

91

Black Box Investigation

A black box contains helpful information about a flight's navigation. It can give investigators clues as to where an explosion occurred and what may have caused it. See how well others can decipher your flight path directions.

- - - - - - - - - - - - -

You'll Need

- 8 tokens, such as small rocks or large Lego bricks
- shoebox
- paper and pen
- 2 volunteers
- stopwatch

1. Write down a summary of a "flight path" through a house, yard, playground, yard, or school building. For example: We flew over _____. Then we passed by _____. Next we saw _____ on our right-hand side, etc. In each recorded area, leave a token like a small rock or a large Lego brick.

2. Place your instructions in the shoebox at the beginning of the "flight path."

3. Have a friend or family member open the shoebox and follow the clues as quickly as she can, gathering each token as she goes and placing it in the box until she reaches the final piece. Time your friend to see how long it takes.

4. Have another friend or family member go through the same course and time his results. Who was better at following the clues?

Further clues led investigators to her son, Jack Graham, who had a record of forgery and theft. His wife was aware that he had placed a gift inside his mom's suitcase, but she did not know what it was. He had also taken out three insurance policies on his mother. This meant that whenever his mom died, he would receive lots of money from the insurance companies. With so much evidence, Graham knew he was caught and confessed to the tragic crime. He was sentenced to death.

BOXES OF INFORMATION

As forensic examiners study and learn about crashes, they gain information that can help create new safety measures. Since the 1960s, every airplane is required to have recording devices, often referred to as *black boxes*. These boxes are not actually black—they are bright orange in order to be found easily after a crash.

One box contains a flight data recorder that records the plane's positions and instrument details. The other recording device is called the *cockpit voice recorder*. It records the last two hours of sound from the cockpit when the pilot and copilot are navigating the plane.

The recorders are positioned near the tail of the plane and made to withstand extreme heat. The boxes even have beacons that activate underwater, sending ultrasound signals for 30 days to increase the chances that investigators will find them. The valuable information learned from the recordings can give investigators information as to what caused the crash.

Since 2002, all passenger ships are also required by law to carry recording devices similar to a plane's black box. A voyage data recorder (VDR) records the voices of those navigating the ship and the details of the ship's movements and positions. The VDR holds at least 12 hours of information.

The VDR might have helped answer questions about the sinking of the *Titanic* had it been available at the time. For many years, the details of the *Titanic*'s sinking left experts puzzled.

David Warren: Inventor of the Black Box

Australian scientist David Warren (1925–2010) invented the first flight recorder in the 1950s. His interest in flight safety may have begun when a tragedy struck Warren's family in 1934: a plane crash left him and three siblings fatherless. The remains of the small plane and passengers were never found. It was believed that the *Miss Hobart*, as the plane was called, crashed in the ocean.

When Warren grew up, he earned a degree in science and a PhD in chemistry. He then worked as a research scientist at the Aeronautical Research Laboratories in Australia. In 1953, he was asked to be part of a team of investigators who would try and solve a mysterious crash. The Comet, the first jetliner passenger aircraft, had crashed on its way to Australia.

During the investigation, Warren realized a recording device could have given them all the information they needed to know. He had recently been to a fair and seen a new invention called a Miniphon, which was a small recorder. He realized a device such as the Miniphon could be used on flights to record the conversations in the cockpit, as well as flight information. This would tell investigators what was happening right before a crash.

When Warren shared his idea with others, it was not received well. He decided he needed to actually make one so that people could get a clear picture of what he imagined. After he built the recorder, he still had difficulty convincing others of its value. Finally, a few countries besides Australia showed interest in it. Then, in 1960, Australia became the first country in the world to make the cockpit voice recorder mandatory.

The recorders on airplanes today still use Warren's basic design. Today the invention that no one was interested in is an invaluable piece of equipment that sits on flights worldwide. The term *black box* denotes an electronic system in a general sense. Somehow the term stuck as the name for the orange flight recorder we know so well.

David Warren with the first black box. *Wikimedia Commons*

On April 12, 1912, the *Titanic* set sail from Southampton, England, on its way to New York. Filled with more than 2,000 passengers and crew, the magnificent vessel was the largest ship in the world at that time. The ship was called "unsinkable" due to its high level of engineering and architecture. The public viewed the *Titanic* as the safest vessel on the seas.

What started out as one of the world's most exciting voyages turned into one of the world's most tragic stories. On the night of April 14, the *Titanic* hit an iceberg in the North Atlantic Ocean. In less than three hours, the safest and largest ship in the world had sunk to the bottom of the sea. The ship was not equipped with enough lifeboats for those on board. More than 1,500 people died. It was a tragedy that left the world in shock. How could this have happened?

The wrecked bow of the *Titanic*. *Wikimedia Commons*

Survivors on lifeboats were picked up by a ship called the *Carpathia*. When the eyewitnesses returned to land, they shared their accounts in an inquiry conducted by the US Senate. A second inquiry followed in the United Kingdom.

An architect who had helped design the *Titanic* took part in one of the inquiries. His name was Edward Wilding. Wilding listened to survivors describe how fast areas of the ship flooded as it sank. Wilding developed mathematical calculations from their testimonies to estimate the time line of the ship's damage. His calculations became the foundation for future forensic investigations.

Eyewitness accounts are important in any investigation, but usually each witness sees things slightly differently. Some of the *Titanic* survivors said they saw the ship break in two pieces as it sank. Others said it sank in one piece. No one could determine which accounts were accurate because the physical evidence of the ship was out of sight, lying somewhere at the bottom of the ocean.

Searches for the ship began in the 1970s when new technology became available, yet no one could locate the sunken ship. It seemed it was an unsolvable case. Finally, in 1985, biologist and naval oceanographer Robert Ballard fulfilled a dream he had carried since childhood: to find the *Titanic*.

Ballard was on a secret mission with the US Navy trying to locate two naval submarines that had disappeared. After he found the subs, the navy allowed him to use its equipment to try and find the *Titanic*. Ballard was given only 12 days to accomplish his mission, though.

Ballard and his team used a self-propelled submarine called *Argo*, equipped with sonar cameras and lights, to find the *Titanic*. Once they found it, they operated *Argo* from aboard a navy vessel and discovered that the hull (main body of the ship) had broken into two pieces. Each piece lay about 2,000 feet (609.6 sq. m) apart on the ocean floor. Now there was physical evidence to prove the witness accounts that the ship had broken in two.

Finding the *Titanic* was just the beginning. What else could be learned about the *Titanic's* sinking? A popular theory was that the iceberg had created a huge gash in the side of the ship, allowing a tremendous influx of water. The portion of the ship that held the answer was hidden beneath mud on the ocean floor. If it could be uncovered, the theory of a huge gash could either be proven or disproven.

A team of scientists, engineers, and architects found the answer on an expedition in 1996. Three divers manned a small underwater vessel called *Nautile*. *Nautile* was equipped with robotic arms that held sonar devices. Sonar could reach the ship through the mud and send acoustic signals to the lab aboard *Nautile*. The signals created images of the damage on the side of the ship. Scientists learned that it was not one big hole that caused the *Titanic's* flooding, but a series of small punctures.

Trying to uncover details about the *Titanic's* sinking does more than satisfy curiosity. Investigations of sunken ships like those of the *Titanic* help scientists and engineers understand what caused a vessel to sink. This information can help them create safer vessels in the future.

The World Trade Center towers, March 2001.
Wikimedia Commons

EVERYTHING CHANGES

Even with all the modern forensic advances, no one was ready for the investigations following September 11, 2001. Foreign terrorists belonging to a group called al-Qaeda took over four American planes, causing them to crash. Two of them smashed into the World Trade Center buildings in New York City. The two buildings were called the Twin Towers.

It was devastating: 2,977 people died and thousands of others were injured. Firefighters, police, and health-care workers came from all over the country to help. All forensic experts of every kind nationwide were called on.

After 9/11, as the attacks came to be referred to, airport security changed. President George W. Bush created the Department of Homeland Security in Washington, DC. Within this department are many agencies that work to keep America safe from terrorism. One of the agencies is called the Transportation Security Administration, or TSA for short.

The TSA instigated many new security measures for airports and airplanes. The cockpit doors of airplanes were reinforced and made to withstand huge amounts of force. Pilots with proper licensing were allowed to carry guns when flying.

Before 9/11, people could go to the boarding gates to say goodbye to loved ones before they entered the plane. The TSA set new rules saying that only those with boarding passes and employees of the airport are allowed near the gates.

Sensitive scanning devices were installed in more places in airports. Body scanners are now also used by airport officials when they feel it is necessary. The scanner is like a wand that is waved over someone's body. It takes a picture like an x-ray that reveals any dangerous hidden items. Computers, phones, and all electronic equipment must be scanned. Some flights also have air marshals. These are officers in plain clothes that join a flight to make sure everything stays safe.

WILDLIFE FORENSICS

One lab is different from all the other forensics labs in the world. This is the US Fish and Wildlife Service (FWS) Forensics Laboratory in Ashland, Oregon. Instead of crimes against people, this lab deals with crimes against wild animals.

In 1979, Ken Goddard was chosen to help start and lead this unusual lab to help tackle the growing wildlife crimes. Goddard had been a chief criminal investigator in California. It took him seven years to receive funds for the lab, see the facility built, and hire experts to work there. Finally, the new forensics lab officially opened in 1989.

As at all forensics labs, experts at the wildlife forensics lab examine and test evidence to be used in court. Some of these crimes involve poaching. Poaching is the illegal killing of animals. There

Ken Goddard. *Courtesy of Ken Goddard, US Fish and Wildlife Service*

are areas where it is not permitted to hunt, such as a national park. Hunting may only be allowed during certain seasons in other areas. People who choose to break the laws protecting animals have committed a serious crime. Evidence from these crimes is sent to the FWS lab to be examined. Evidence might include tire track evidence, weapons and ammunition, or animal parts.

Other crimes against wildlife involve endangered animals. Animals such as the black rhino, sea turtle, and bald eagle fall into this category. There are so few of them left that they are in danger of becoming extinct. Criminals make billions of dollars each year from killing and selling exotic and endangered animals or their parts. Often, the money made from them funds rebel groups, organized crime, and terrorist groups.

Ivory from elephant tusks has long been a valued commodity for its beauty. Decorative items and jewelry are made with the pearly white material. The United States has made it illegal to import ivory from elephant tusks in order to protect the rapid killing of these animals. There are other types of ivory from sperm whale teeth, walrus tusks, warthog tusks, and other animals. Different laws apply to different species. But how do the scientists at the FWS lab know which type of ivory they are looking at or even if it is ivory at all?

First, UV lights can reveal if the white specimen is real or an ivory copy made with resin or plastic. If it is real ivory, the scientist must then determine which animal it is from. Scientists use an electron microscope to examine the patterns

Examining an elephant tusk.
Courtesy of Ken Goddard, US Fish and Wildlife Service

inside the tusk. These patterns are called *Schreger lines*. If the Schreger lines are a certain angle, this will help the forensic examiner determine whether the tusk is from an elephant. To learn if it is an Asian elephant or an African elephant, the examiner will grind a small part of the tusk into powder and test it for DNA.

These are just a few of the hundreds of types of tests performed at the FWS lab that help assist investigations all over the United States and beyond. To find out more about this interesting forensics lab, you can visit its website: www.fws .gov/lab/stories.php.

7 REACHING BACK AND HEADING FORWARD

Think back on all the crimes that occurred before the discovery of DNA and other forensic technologies. Without proper forensic tools, many of them were left unsolved. In some cases, innocent people may have been convicted of crimes they did not commit, or a dangerous criminal may have been left out on the streets. What if forensic scientists could take the new forensic technologies and use them to solve cases in the past? That is what some investigators are doing. They are called *cold case investigators*.

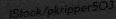

iStock/pkripper503

J. Warner Wallace: Cold Case Homicide Detective

J. Warner Wallace is a cold case homicide detective with the Torrance Police Department in California. Although he dreamed of being a police officer like his dad when he was a child, he had other ideas when he entered college. His natural artistic gifts led him to earn a degree in design. When he decided it would be hard to make a living as an artist, he returned to school and earned a master's degree in architecture. He landed a job as an architect but decided designing buildings was not a good fit either. There was something about the work that felt a bit empty. He wanted to do something to help people. That's when Wallace decided to follow in his dad's footsteps and become a cop.

During a three-month recovery from an injury, Wallace was unable to do his regular work. He decided to pull one of his dad's unsolved cases off the shelf and see if he could solve it. After he and his team solved it successfully, he realized how much he enjoyed doing it. He decided to form a cold case team, something his department did not have at the time.

J. Warner Wallace.
Courtesy J. Warner Wallace

"Often, people think cold cases are all solved by DNA evidence," says Detective Wallace, "but that is most often not true." In fact, he likes tackling cases where DNA is not available. He finds it more challenging "doing it the old-fashioned way." Also, DNA analysis is expensive even when investigators use ancestry databases. The police must pay these companies money to access their databases.

What does a cold case investigator's day look like? Wallace heads into the office and pulls a cold case report off the shelf from the case reports division. Sometimes, with old cases, there are many reports about the same case in different areas. He collects them all and puts them in one notebook. He also collects any evidence that was secured from the crime scene and carefully rebags it all. Everything now feels like this is a new case, his case. Now he will examine it with a fresh set of eyes.

If there are witnesses still alive, he may want to interview them. At some point, he will want to talk with the suspect too. At first, though, he does not want the suspect to know the case has reopened. He wants to maximize the chances of getting a bad guy to tell the truth. "It is not about getting him to say something to win a case," says Detective Wallace. "Investigation is about searching for the truth."

Wallace uses a special forensic technique when reading witness and suspect interviews. It is called Forensic Statement Analysis. This type of training allows him to look closely at the choice of words a person uses. He is able to pinpoint certain words or phrases that reveal deception. Wallace also uses this same forensic technique when talking in person with witnesses and suspects. Wallace says this is one of the top ways he discovers the clues he needs.

As he examines all the case information, he is searching for missing puzzle pieces. He works closely with the district attorney (DA). The DA is the one who decides which cases have enough evidence to file. The DA might help Wallace understand he needs a few more pieces of evidence or certain types of evidence in order to bring the case to trial.

As Wallace moves forward searching for evidence, he looks at every detail. "Everything becomes evidence," says Wallace, "absolutely everything! There are two types of evidence: direct evidence, which is the witnesses, and indirect evidence, which is everything else."

One of the pieces of evidence left from a cold case Wallace was working on was a piece of foam. Wallace wondered where it had come from. It wasn't from something in the home . . . it must have come from the suspect. When he examined a photo of the suspect, he noticed he was wearing a pair of work boots. Wallace wondered if the foam came from the boots. He asked if the boots had been secured as evidence, and sure enough, they had. Wallace found an area in one of the boots that had foam filling missing. He contacted an FBI shoe expert who confirmed the piece of foam had come from the boot. This became important evidence revealing the suspect had been at the crime scene.

One of the most important things to remember as a cold case detective is to "not be a know-it-all," says Wallace. "Don't jump to conclusions. Let the evidence tell you what it is."

"Hot on the trail" is a term that means detectives are close to catching a criminal. They have found clues that are leading them swiftly to a suspect. When a case has hit a dead end and exhausted all leads, it is referred to as a *cold case*. All the information about the case is put on a shelf and sits there while other "hot" cases are solved. Cold case investigators pull the cases off the shelf and reinvestigate them.

WHEN COLD BECOMES HOT

Many cases are reopened that have questionable convictions or remain unsolved. One of them was a murder that occurred in 1997. Nevest Coleman, a groundskeeper for the Chicago White Sox baseball team, **was** brought in for questioning after the murder of his friend Antwinica Bridgeman. During the questioning, he signed a statement admitting his guilt. Back then, police interrogations were not recorded. Coleman later claimed that police pressured him into a confession, promising his release.

Instead of being released, Coleman was sent to prison for life. Without the signed confession, there was not enough evidence for a conviction, but with a confession, no other evidence was needed. In 2016, DNA testing was conducted on evidence from the case. The DNA pointed to another man with a criminal record as the murderer. Coleman was released after serving 20 years in prison.

WHAT REALLY HAPPENED?

DNA is useful not only in solving cold cases but also in solving mysteries regarding the deaths of famous people. Nicholas Romanov was the tsar, or emperor, of Russia, crowned in 1896 as Nicholas II. He and his wife, Alexandra, had five children: four girls and a boy. In July 1918, a group called the Bolsheviks took over Russia, leading the country into communism. As part of their takeover, they secretly executed the entire Romanov family and disposed of their bodies. But no one knew if the whole family had been killed or if perhaps some members had escaped. Many wondered if they were alive and hiding somewhere.

In the 1970s, a grave was found with remains believed to be those of the Romanov family, but it was kept secret. It wasn't until 1991 that the discovery was made known to the public. Forensic scientists from the United Kingdom joined specialists from Russia to try and figure out who the skeletons belonged to. Could DNA testing work on bones that were so aged?

The forensic scientists were able to extract very small amounts of DNA from the bones. When very little DNA is available, mitochondrial DNA testing is done. Mitochondrial DNA is passed from a mother to her children.

In order to test the mitochondrial DNA from the bones, scientists needed to compare it with DNA samples of other living Romanov family members. They took blood samples from Alexandra's relatives and also from Nicholas's family on his mother's side. They learned that the remains were most assuredly Nicholas II, his wife Alexandra, and three of their daughters. The other remains were thought to belong to their four servants.

Rumors and stories now circulated about the two missing Romanov children. Many people came forward claiming they were the son, Alexei, or one of the daughters who had escaped. All claims were eventually proven false.

Still, the lingering question remained: what had happened to the other family members? Finally, in 2007, archaeologists found another grave near the first one. After DNA mitochondrial testing was conducted, it was confirmed that the new grave contained the two missing Romanov family members, Alexei and one of the sisters. The mystery was finally solved.

KING TUT MYSTERY

An area in Egypt called the Valley of the Kings contains underground tombs of ancient Egyptian pharaohs. In 1922, archaeologist Howard Carter discovered the tomb of King Tutankhamen, often referred to as King Tut. The tomb contained thousands of treasures including a gold mask, which covered the mummified face of the young king. Tut was just nine years old when he took the throne, and he died when he was only 19.

Curiosity stirred as to why he died so young. Was he murdered so someone else could take his throne? Maybe he was struck down by a disease of some kind. At the time there was really no way to answer these questions.

In 2005, Egyptian archaeologist Zahi Hawass wanted to solve the mystery of King Tut's death using modern science. He and his team carefully removed King Tut's remains from the tomb. They placed the mummy inside a CT scanning machine that took about 1,500 x-ray pictures of the mummy. The team believed they were about to solve the oldest murder mystery anyone had ever solved.

Before the scan, many specialists hypothesized that King Tut had died from a blow to the head. They came to this conclusion because of a hole on the side of the skull. The CT scan revealed that the hole was not caused by foul play or by an accident. Instead, the hole had been created for embalming fluid to be placed in King Tut's body. This was not an unusual practice for ancient embalming methods. The CT scan even revealed areas where the embalming fluid had dripped down from the hole.

The CT scan also showed no signs of a disease present in King Tut's body when he died. Although he had suffered from bouts of malaria and a club-foot, it was clear that a disease had not killed him. What they did see was a severely broken left leg and evidence of infection. Thanks to the CT scan, scientists believe the infection was the actual culprit that caused his death.

Later, a team of scientists joined with Dr. Hawass to study King Tut's DNA. Extracting DNA from the bones of ancient Egyptian mummies had never been done before. They were not sure if it would be successful. They wanted to compare the DNA with DNA from 16 other ancient mummies in tombs surrounding King Tut's. They were

King Tut's burial mask.
Roland Unger, Wikimedia Commons

interested to see if any of the other mummies were related to him.

It worked! They found King Tut's father, grandmother, and a mummy they believe to be his mother.

SCANNING YOUR IDENTITY

Even though DNA is the most powerful unique characteristic to date, there are always new evolving forms of identification. One of them is biometrics. Biometrics is the use of digital technology to identify a person's unique characteristics.

A facial recognition system creates a map of the features on a face from a video or photo. The results are compared with faces in a database. Often, the results simply narrow the search down to several similar faces.

In some areas in the United States, mobile face recognition systems are now being used in police cars. A police officer can take a photo of an offender who does not have an ID and then compare it with those in the facial recognition database to see if one matches.

The human iris. *iStock/metamorworks*

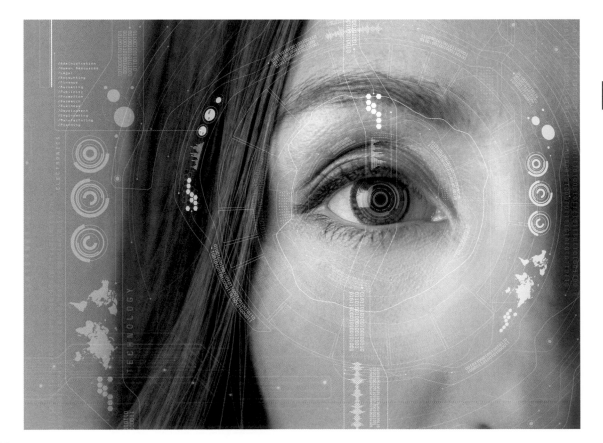

Eye scanning is another form of biometric identification. The colored part of a person's eye is called the *iris*. Each person's iris is unique in much the same way a fingerprint is. The iris has swirls and ridges, which create unique patterns. Laser eye-scanning equipment contains algorithms that measure and map the patterns of the iris. An algorithm is simply a task that a computer system is programmed to perform. Then the scanned information can be put into an iris database.

Other forms of biometrics include scanned fingerprints, handprints, and tattoos. Voice algorithms measure the unique qualities of an individual's voice and speech. Gait algorithms record the way a person walks. Algorithms are underway that even calculate each person's unique perspiration.

CASE SOLVED

Biometric databases are helpful in solving cold cases, such as a murder that occurred in 1978. When Carroll Bonnet was killed, latent fingerprints were found in his apartment. Investigators compared them with fingerprints in local and state files, but a match was never found. The case turned cold.

In 2008, the clearest latent print from the crime scene was scanned into the IAFIS (Integrated Automated Fingerprint Identification System). This huge FBI fingerprint database was not available in 1978, when the murder was committed. Within hours, several possible matches turned up. A specialist analyzed the prints and found that one matched exactly. It belonged to a man named Jerry

Forensics and the Unknown Soldier

The Arlington National Cemetery in Arlington County, Virginia, contains more than 14,000 veterans' graves. On top of a hill there sits a tomb that is guarded 24 hours a day by armed service members. It is called the Tomb of the Unknown Soldier.

Four soldiers were buried there at one time, and now there are three. The three remaining soldiers are from three different wars: World War I, World War II, and the Korean War. They are buried there to commemorate all the soldiers from these wars whose bodies were never identified or are still missing.

The Tomb of the Unknown Soldier. *Kyler Becker, Wikimedia Commons*

In 1984, a Vietnam soldier's remains were added to the tomb site. This was the same year that Alec Jeffreys made his DNA discovery. It was much too early for DNA to be used as a form of accepted identification. Other types of forensic analysis were conducted on the serviceman's remains, but many experts questioned how they were performed. Later, sloppy handling of evidence would also be discovered.

There were certain items found with the remains, including a life raft, parachute, flight suit pieces, and holster. This physical evidence led to the conclusion that the serviceman flew an aircraft. Because of the location in Vietnam where the airman's remains were found and the evidence with it, many strongly believed they belonged to 24-year-old Michael J. Blassie. His plane had been shot down near the crash site in 1972. Even so, the remains were tagged "unidentified."

By 1991, DNA was a widely used means of identification. The Blassie family asked for the remains to be exhumed and tested. A mitochondrial DNA test was performed on a few samples of bones. This type of DNA testing requires only a small amount of DNA and is inherited through the maternal side of the family. The exhumed soldier's DNA was compared with a DNA sample from Blassie's mom, and it matched. No one could argue with the evidence now.

Blassie's remains were taken to Jefferson Barracks Cemetery in St. Louis, Missouri. His grave was finally marked with his name. No other Vietnam serviceman's remains took the place of Blassie's at the Tomb of the Unknown Soldier.

above: **Personal items found with the remains of 1st Lt. Michael Blassie.** *Patricia Blassie*

right: **Michael Blassie's life raft.** *Patricia Blassie*

Watson who was about to be released from prison after serving time for a burglary.

Forensic scientists extracted DNA from a hair strand that had been kept as evidence from the case. The DNA from the hair root matched Watson's blood sample DNA. He was found guilty 33 long years after committing the crime and sentenced to life in prison.

DNA DATABASES

Every state is required to submit the DNA of certain types of criminals to databases. The FBI's database is called the Combined DNA Index System (CODIS). It combines DNA from local, state, and national levels. Investigators can compare a DNA sample from a crime they are working on to DNA in the CODIS database to see if there is a match.

Another method of DNA matching is done by using autosomal DNA. This kind of DNA is inherited by both parents. Using a public ancestry DNA database, investigators can find family members who share the DNA. This can then help them track down close relatives and then an individual.

In 1979, an 18-year-old woman named Michelle Marie Martinko was killed in Cedar Rapids, Iowa. The perpetrator was never found. After all investigations were exhausted, the case turned cold. In 2006, new technology helped cold case investigators retrieve the killer's DNA from crime scene evidence on file. When the DNA sample was put through the CODIS database, though, no match was found.

Newer technology in 2017 finally helped solve the case. First, the DNA was sent to a lab that created a DNA phenotype. A phenotype is a way to predict a person's physical appearance. Specialists were able to examine the genetic traits within the DNA to create a composite, or picture, of the suspect.

The phenotype pictures are not exact replicas of a person, but they resemble the person's general appearance. Specialists determined certain traits of the suspect such as blond hair and blue or green eyes. A picture was made of his likeness at 25 and another at age 50. Next, detectives shared the pictures with the public, hoping that someone might recognize him.

Investigators also searched public ancestry databases to see if they could find a matching relative's DNA. They found a far-removed cousin who eventually led them to three brothers and finally to the perpetrator, who was named Jerry Lynn Burns. After 37 years, the case was closed. Burns was sentenced to life in prison.

Another new development in DNA analysis is called *rapid DNA testing*. It usually takes weeks or months for officials to receive DNA test results. Rapid DNA tests are much faster and automated. A DNA sample can be compared with other DNA in the CODIS system in just a few hours without any human technician involved in the process. Rapid DNA tests are allowed to be used when a person arrested has committed a serious offense. Then officers can learn right away if the individual in custody has committed other crimes. This can help keep dangerous criminals from being released to the streets.

The Shroud of Turin is the most studied artifact in the world, and yet it still remains a mystery. The shroud is a rectangular linen cloth about 14.5 feet (4.4 m) long and 3.5 feet (1.07 m) wide. Since 1578 it has been housed in the Cathedral of St. John the Baptist in Turin, Italy. The cloth contains a faint mirror image, front and back, of a crucified man. Many people believe it is the burial cloth of the Jesus of Nazareth portrayed in the New Testament. Others claim it is a fake. What does science say?

In 1976, scientists John Jackson and Eric Jumper used a VP-8 Image Analyzer on photo images of the shroud. They discovered distinct properties of depth that normal photos do not contain. This led them to conclude that a real human had been wrapped in the cloth at the time the unusual image was formed.

This discovery led a group of 33 scientists to form a team to study the shroud. They came from science labs across the United States, including two from NASA. The team was referred to as the Shroud of Turin Research Project (STURP). About 25 members of the group traveled to Italy while the others remained at home waiting for data to study upon their return.

STURP's mission was to scientifically determine how the image on the shroud was created. They were given permission to set up a temporary lab inside the royal palace in Turin for five days and nights. Using the most up-to-date equipment at that time, they studied the shroud and carefully collected data for 120 hours. One of the STURP

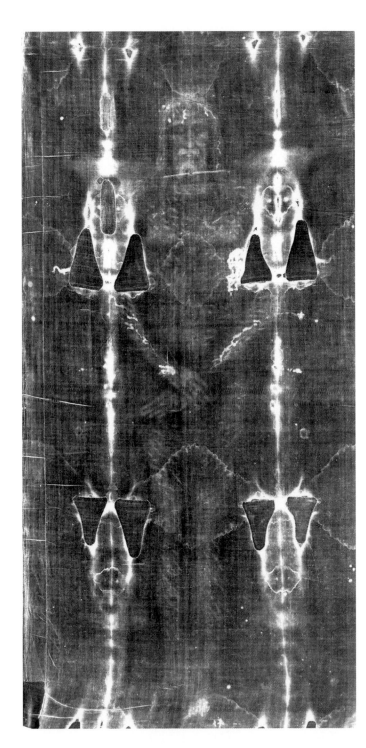

The Shroud of Turin.
Courtesy of Barrie Schwortz

107

Barrie Schwortz.
Courtesy of Barrie Schwortz

team members was Barrie Schwortz, a professional scientific photographer.

"My main job was to document the entire shroud research project using photography. I also created photographic maps. Each analyzed area was noted with small numbered magnets designed so they would not contaminate the cloth. I photographed each place on the cloth where data was taken from."

The STURP team concluded that the image was not made with paint or pigments and that the red stains were blood. Chemical tests revealed hemoglobin, a material of blood, in the stains.

Schwortz was most amazed after seeing the cloth under ultraviolet lights. "On many of the bloodstains, a serum halo was seen. Serum is the watery part of the blood that separates from red and white blood cells. This is exactly how blood would react as it flowed onto the cloth. This information was only visible under ultraviolet light, though, a thing a medieval forger would have no knowledge of."

A second hypothesis held by some in the scientific community was that the image on the shroud may have been created by heating up a sculpted image and transferring it to the linen as a scorch. The STURP team needed to test this idea.

"The shroud was damaged by a fire in 1532 and has scorches, holes, and patches on each side from the fire. We were able to use ultraviolet fluorescence photography to compare the known scorched areas with the image of the man. Under UV lights, the known scorched areas turned red around the edges because of the heat that formed them. The other areas of the cloth were green. The image of the crucified man did not fluoresce at all."

Another thought was that the image was created with photography. "Obviously, the image was formed before photography was invented," explains Schwortz. "A medieval form of photography could have only been accomplished using silver. STURP found no silver anywhere on the shroud. It would have been impossible to have removed it all if it had been used."

In 1988, three laboratories outside of STURP received permission to take samples from the shroud. Each lab took a piece of one sample to study using carbon 14 dating. The testing determined that the shroud dated from between 1260 and 1390. This meant that the shroud must be a medieval fake.

The STURP team questioned how the tests were performed. Instead of using three separate pieces from different areas of the cloth, the three labs used only one sample from one place on the shroud. STURP scientist Raymond Rogers stated that the 1988 sample was from an area that was patched from fire damage after 1532.

For now, the question STURP sought to answer remains a mystery. How was the image on the shroud formed? STURP continued tests on the data after their return from Italy. They released all their findings in 1981. The scientific results, photos, and articles about the shroud can be found on Schwortz's website: www.shroud.com.

LET ME SEE YOUR HAND

Unique characteristics that each of us possess are constantly being discovered and explored. An unusual type of identification was developed by forensic anthropologist Sue Black and her team in Scotland. They realized that each person's hands contain individual information. Perhaps a criminal's face did not appear on a video or photo, but maybe his or her hand was captured.

Dr. Black and her team developed a system of analyzing the unique vein patterns of a hand. Many other characteristics of hands are also unique, such as knuckle skin folds. These vein patterns and skin crease patterns are formed in the

Unique Hands

The vein pattern in a hand can usually be seen pretty clearly. Unique vein patterns are one of the many distinguishing characteristics that can link a specific individual to a crime. See if you can match the vein patterns.

You'll Need

- 3 or 4 volunteers
- camera
- printer
- tracing paper
- pen or marker

1. Take photographs of a family member's hand or hands of friends. Have each person first make a tight fist while you photograph the back of the hand, trying to capture any vein patterns.

2. Now take a second photo of the hand laid flat.

3. Finally, for a third photo, pose the hand in some other way that can help capture the vein pattern the best.

4. Print the photos and enlarge them if needed. Trace the vein patterns you see on the photos using a pen or marker and tracing paper.

5. Place the marked photos together and write down three unique features for each hand, when looked at together.

6. Take the tracings and observations and compare them to the actual hands. See if you can match which vein pattern belong to which person.

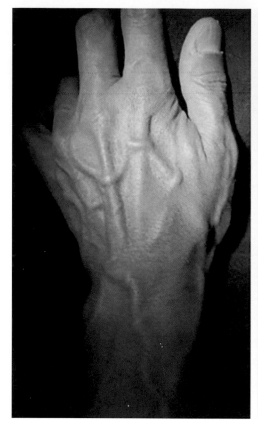
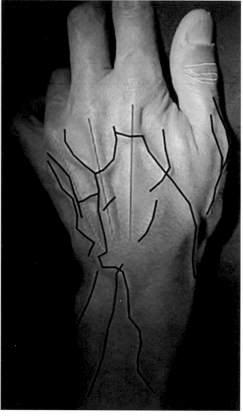

Hand patterns.
Prof. Dame Sue Black

or county. Others are state or national databases. Some databases are maintained by law enforcement agencies, others by commercial companies.

Investigators can compare sample evidence they have collected from a crime scene and electronically compare it with samples in a database. For example, if an unknown shoe print has been lifted from a floor, the sole pattern can be compared with known database sole patterns. If a match is found, an investigator learns what type of shoe created the print.

The FBI maintains numerous databases for investigators to reference. The Integrated Automated Fingerprint Identification System (IAFIS) was developed in 1999. The IAFIS contained fingerprints of people who had been arrested. These prints were collected from city, state, and federal agencies. Many of the IAFIS fingerprints were also collected from people for other reasons not related to crime. For instance, sometimes an employer requires a background check before hiring a new employee. The background check includes fingerprinting. These fingerprints were also put into IAFIS.

In 2011, a new system replaced IAFIS. It is called the Next Generation Identification (NGI) system. This new database contains all that IAFIS did and more. Other biometric information includes palm prints, iris scans, and facial recognition. Police officers can use a mobile fingerprint device at the time of arrest, take a print, compare it with prints in NGI, and receive results in seconds.

The possibility of having information of all kinds stored in one place may be in the future.

womb and never change throughout life. Algorithms have also been developed that map the vein patterns in the hand and even in the fingers.

ALL IN ONE PLACE

Databases are an important part of forensic science. There are hundreds of different databases in the United States alone. There are databases filled with files of fingerprints, DNA, paint chips, fiber information, glass evidence, tread marks, thumbprints, ballistics, and more. Some of these databases are local ones, perhaps covering a city

Every type of imaginable database could be referenced easily and quickly, saving huge amounts of time. This information would include much more than just evidence, biometric identification, and DNA. It could also include information on how certain cases have been solved and different types of investigation techniques.

THIS IS NO GAME

In a criminal trial, often jurors are shown photos, videos, and sketches of a crime scene. While this is helpful, it is not the same as actually seeing the scene of the crime in person. If only there could be a device like a virtual reality video game where jurors could enter the world of the crime scene. In this way, jurors could see the actual undisturbed view the same way investigators originally found it.

Mehzeb Chowdhury, a forensic science researcher, was inspired by the NASA rover unit to create a machine called the MABMAT. Like the NASA rover robot, the MABMAT can move around taking 360-degree photos and videos. Then, using the MABMAT app on an iPhone or computer along with an inexpensive adapter headset, jurors can enter the crime scene and look around. They can view the scene from any angle, look side to side, or search up and down. They can even zoom in for a closer look at evidence whenever they need to.

Another important opportunity the MABMAT gives jurors is the opportunity to experience different people's perspectives. This would mean that a juror could view the scene from the victim's position and then from the criminal's viewpoint and then from a police officer's line of sight.

Virtual reality might also be the way autopsies are routinely performed in the future. Imaging technology like CT and MRI scans can help experts view the inside of a corpse while leaving the body intact. A few countries are already using this type of autopsy imaging.

A Swiss forensic team led by Michael Thali, has developed an invention to aid the virtual autopsies called the Virtobot. The Virtobot has a robotic arm that can insert a small needle to take tiny tissue samples from the body where needed. A liquid dye can also be inserted in blood vessels to reveal information that might not be accessible in a regular autopsy.

IMAGINE THE FUTURE

Testing evidence takes time, time that may be crucial in finding a suspect or victim. In the future, robots may become the way to save time in the lab. Robotic devices could test many samples—like blood—at one time and much faster.

Mass spectrometry is a process that gives scientists information about the molecular makeup of a substance. It is often used in forensic toxicology and arson investigations. It can now be used to collect clues about a person, too.

After an individual has touched a surface like a phone, a mass spectrometer can test the molecules left from the hand. Information such as what makeup the person wears, or medications he

Assemble a Forensic Kit

Now that you have learned the history and science of crime solving, you can assemble a forensic kit for your own investigations. Use a plastic or cardboard box to gather your supplies. Below are suggestions to start with. Think of other things you can add.

You'll Need

- large and small plastic baggies for evidence
- small plastic containers for delicate evidence
- masking tape and permanent markers to label evidence containers
- plastic gloves
- goggles
- magnifying glass
- ink pad for fingerprints
- note cards for fingerprints
- tweezers for collecting small pieces of evidence
- clear packaging tape for lifting prints
- notepad for making notes
- measuring tape
- flashlight
- yellow crime scene tape
- black chunky crayon for making print rubbings
- tracing paper

1. Gather the items above that you can find.
2. Add anything from activities you have already performed—your Shoe Print Database, your Tire Tread Prints, and more.

or she takes, or even certain liquids an individual drinks can all be revealed. These clues can give investigators important leads concerning a suspect and might be used more widely in the future.

Samples needed for DNA analysis keep getting smaller. At one time, a quarter-sized amount of fluid was needed to obtain DNA. Now a method called *touch DNA* is emerging. When a person touches something, skin cells are left behind. DNA can now be examined from these tiny cells. New knowledge about the makeup of DNA and genes is growing fast and is sure to affect forensics in the future.

How else will forensics change in the years ahead? Advances in science and technology will mean greater accuracy in testing and time savings for investigations. New forms of biometric identification will surely emerge. Medical discoveries will help provide greater understanding of other unique attributes for identification.

With evolving digital technology, criminals will develop new forms of cybercrime, and new digital forensics will respond to combat it. Perhaps satellites and space will play a role as well. One thing is for sure: as in the past, imaginative scientists will lead the way.

GLOSSARY

algorithms a set of calculations a computer is programmed to perform

alternate light source light used at crime scenes and labs that reveals hidden evidence that cannot be seen with regular lighting

anthropometric the scientific study of measurements of the body

arson unlawfully and deliberately setting fire to property

ATF lab (Bureau of Alcohol, Tobacco, Firearms, and Explosives) federal agency that examines explosives evidence

autopsy an examination of a body to discover the cause of death

ballistics the study of firearms and ammunition

Bertillon system a system of measuring an individual's body for the purpose of identification

biometric identifiers human characteristics that can be measured by computer software in order to identify an individual

blood spatter small particles of blood

bloodstain pattern analysis the scientific study of bloodstains at a crime scene

blood type a classification of blood groups

Body Farm the forensic anthropology center in Knoxville, Tennessee, dedicated to researching body decomposition

Bow Street Runners a professional police force in London started by Henry and John Fielding in 1749

cadaver a corpse studied by the medical or scientific community

chain of custody the way physical evidence is documented as it is transferred from person to person

chromatography a scientific method of separating components of a mixture

circumstantial evidence evidence that by itself cannot prove something

cleansuit a protective covering worn when collecting evidence in a crime scene

CODIS (Combined DNA Index System) an FBI database containing DNA profiles

cold case a criminal case that has not been solved

comparison microscope two microscopes that are connected by an optical bridge in order to view different pieces of evidence at the same time

composite drawing a suspect drawing created by a forensic artist from a witness description

computer virus a code written to alter a computer's normal operating systems

computer worm a malicious computer program that spreads from one computer to another

conclusive evidence evidence that can establish a fact

contaminated evidence crime scene evidence that has been altered in some way from its original form

counterfeit a copy made of something with the intention to deceive someone

CT scan a computerized machine that takes a series of extremely detailed x-rays of a human body from different angles

cyanoacrylate adhesive (super glue) used as a vapor to adhere to latent fingerprints in order to make them visible

cybercrime a crime that involves one or more computers

cybersecurity analyst a person whose job is to protect the computers in an organization from malicious software

crime scene the area in which a crime takes place as well as other areas associated with the crime

database a computerized collection of information that investigators can search through

DNA (deoxyribonucleic acid) a distinctive material that is unique to all individuals and present in almost every cell of the body

DNA phenotype an image of a person's face created from DNA information

entomology the scientific study of insects

evidence information or physical items that give validity or proof of something

facial recognition technology used to measure an individual's facial characteristics for identification purposes

facial reconstruction sculpting or using computer software to create a three-dimensional face from skeletal remains

FBI (Federal Bureau of Investigation) federal agency that oversees federal investigations

fingerprint the unique markings left from the ridges of an individual's fingertips that can be used to identify the individual

fire patterns shapes formed from a fire that are examined by fire investigators

flashover the instant a fire suddenly spreads rapidly because of the extreme heat

fluorescent powder powder used to reveal latent fingerprints

forensic anthropology analysis of the human skeleton for the purposes of identification and crime solving

forensic odontology the scientific study of teeth

forensic pathologist examiner who performs autopsies in suspicious deaths

forensic photography photos taken to record crime scenes and evidence

forensics science used to help solve crimes.

forgery creating a copy of a piece of artwork or a document in order to deceive

fraud criminal means used to obtain finances

FWS (US Fish and Wildlife Service Forensics Laboratory) started by Ken Goddard in 1979 to help solve crimes against wildlife

hacking gaining access to a computer without authorization

handwriting analysis examination of the characteristics of a handwriting sample in order to evaluate its authenticity

Henry Classification System a method of classifying fingerprints based on unique patterns

IAFIS (Integrated Automated Fingerprint Identification System) a database of fingerprints that began in 1999 for fingerprint identification

iris recognition a biometric form of identification that measures the unique patterns of the iris

latent prints fingerprints that are not visible to the naked eye

Locard's Exchange Principle the principle of modern forensics coined by Edmond Locard that states, "Every contact leaves a trace"

MABMAT a robotic machine that can take 360-degree pictures and videos of crime scenes

Marsh test a method created by James Marsh for detecting minute traces of arsenic

mass spectrometry a technique used to measure the mass of a particular substance

mitochondrial DNA DNA that is inherited from the mother

mug shot a photo taken of someone after he or she has been arrested

NGI (Next Generation Identification) an FBI biometric database

odontology the scientific study of teeth

patent prints fingerprints that are visible to the naked eye

pattern evidence a print left at a crime scene that can be examined and compared

physical evidence evidence collected for analysis such as fingerprints, fibers, glass, and other materials

Pinkerton's National Detective Agency a detective agency in Chicago, Illinois, that was founded in 1850 by Allan Pinkerton

precipitin test a test that can determine if blood is from an animal or human

presumptive test an initial test on a piece of evidence to determine if further tests are required

probative evidence evidence that is sufficient to prove something

rogues' gallery a collection of photos of persons who have been arrested

serology the scientific study of human fluids such as blood

Scotland Yard headquarters of the Metropolitan Police in London

search patterns different methods of searching for evidence

Sherlock Holmes a character in a series of novels by Arthur Conan Doyle

Teichmann test a test that confirms if a substance is blood or not

toolmark a type of mark made by a tool at a crime scene that can be examined by a forensic scientist

touch DNA tiny amounts of DNA that can be examined from very few skin cells

toxicology the scientific study of poisons and their effects

trace evidence small pieces of evidence

unknown sample evidence whose origin an investigator does not know

UV light ultraviolet lights used to illuminate evidence that might otherwise lie hidden

vein patterns the unique layout of veins on a person's hands

Virtobot a machine invented by Michael Thali to assist in virtual autopsies

virtual autopsy a method of using CT scans and other technology to examine a corpse

RESOURCES

MUSEUMS

Sherlock Holmes Museum
221b Baker Stret
Maryleborne, London NW1 6XE
United Kingdom
A museum set up as though it is the home and office of the fictional character Sherlock Homes from author Conan Doyle's novels.

Smithsonian National Museum of Natural History
10th Street and Constitution Avenue
Washington, DC 20560
A national history museum with a variety of exhibits including anthropology.

Mob Museum
300 Stewart Avenue
Las Vegas, NV 89101
A museum about organized crime in the 1930s.

National Law Enforcement Museum
444 E Street NW
Washington, DC 20001
Includes interactive exhibits such as a decision-making training simulator, forensics evidence gathering, and 9-1-1 emergency operator dispatch experience.

The FBI Experience
J. Edgar Hoover Building
935 Pennsylvania Avenue NW
Washington, DC 20535
A self-guided tour of FBI history.

WEBSITES

FBI Kids: www.fbi.gov/fbi-kids
Explain That Stuff: www.explainthatstuff.com/forensicscience.html
Forensic Anthropology at the Smithsonian: https://naturalhistory.si.edu/education/teaching-resources/written-bone/forensic-anthropology/forensic-anthropology-smithsonian

Forensic Science Simplified: www.forensicsciencesimplified.org/

Forensic Science: https://science.howstuffworks.com/forensic-science-channel.htm

Detective Mysteries: www.squiglysplayhouse.com/BrainTeasers/Detective.php

Crime Museum: www.crimemuseum.org

Virtual Exhibit on Forensic Science: www.virtualmuseum.ca/sgc-cms/expositions-exhibitions/detective-investigator/en/index.html

SPECIAL ANNIVERSARIES

January 6: Annual date celebrating the birthday of Sherlock Holmes started in 1934 by a Sherlock Holmes society called the Baker Street Irregulars

September: National Forensic Science Week is one week each September celebrating forensic science contributions https://forensicscienceweek.org

NOTES

1: WHAT IS FORENSIC SCIENCE?

"There is nothing": Song Ci, *The Washing Away of Wrongs*, ed. M. Clement Hall, trans. Herbert A. Giles (Lulu, 2010).

2. FORENSIC SCIENCE IN THE 19TH CENTURY

"every contact leaves a trace": National Forensic Science Technology Center, "Principles of Trace Evidence," accessed September 21, 2021, http://www.forensicsciencesimplified.org/trace/principles.html.

3. THE MANY FORMS OF IDENTIFICATION

"[Bones] don't forget": *A Conversation With . . .* , season 5, episode 501, "Clyde Snow," aired August 8, 2012, on OETA, https://videos.oeta.tv/video/oetas-conversation-clyde-snow/.

"I'm anti-homicide": Bryan Painter, *Oklahoman*, February 19, 2010.

4. MODERN FORENSICS MOVES FORWARD

"I like to think of tire footprints": "The Designer's Craft Used to Solve Murders," *New York Times*, January 4, 1982.

5. NOT THE USUAL FORENSICS: FORGERIES AND CYBERCRIMES

"Think of your computer" through *"Be careful"*: Tony Fullman, author interview, August 2020.

7. REACHING BACK AND HEADING FORWARD

"Often, people think" through *"not be a know-it-all"*: J. Warner Wallace, author interview, September 2020.

"My main job was" through *"Obviously, the image"*: Barrie Schwortz, author interview, September 2020.

SELECTED BIBLIOGRAPHY

*Books suitable for children

Ball, William, and Jon Jefferson. *Beyond the Body Farm: A Legendary Bone Detective Explores Murders, Mysteries, and the Revolution in Forensic Science.* New York: William Morrow, 2007.

*Barnes-Svarney, Patricia, and Thomas E. Svarney. *The Handy Forensic Science Answer Book.* Canton, MI: Visible Ink Press, 2019.

Bell, Suzanne. *Crime and Circumstance: Investigating the History of Forensic Science.* Westport, CT: Praeger, 2008.

*Birmingham, Maria. *Biometrics: Your Body and the Science of Security.* Toronto: Owlkids Books, 2017.

Black, Sue M. *All That Remains: A Renowned Forensic Scientist on Death, Mortality, and Solving Crimes.* New York: Arcade Publishing, 2019.

*Crewe, Sabrina. *A History of the FBI.* Broomall, PA: Mason Crest Publishers, 2009.

*Heinrichs, Ann. *Fire Investigator.* Ann Arbor, MI: Cherry Lake Publishing, 2009.

*Heos, Bridget. *Blood, Bullets, and Bones: The Story of Forensic Science from Sherlock Holmes to DNA.* New York: Balzar+Bray, 2016.

*Hopping, Lorraine Jean. *Bone Detective: The Story of Forensic Anthropologist Diane France.* New York: Franklin Watts, 2005.

Joyce, Christopher, and Eric Stover. *Witnesses from the Grave: The Stories Bones Tell.* Boston: Little, Brown, 1992.

*Kallner, Donna Jackson. *The Wildlife Detectives.* Boston: Houghton Mifflin, 2000.

Koff, Clea. *The Bone Woman.* New York: Random House Trade Paperbacks, 2005.

McCrery, Nigel. *Silent Witnesses: The Often Gruesome but Always Fascinating History of Forensic Science.* Chicago: Chicago Review Press, 2014.

McDermid, Val. *Forensics: What Bugs, Burns, Prints, DNA, and More Tell Us About Crime.* New York: Grove Press, 2014.

Owen, David. *Hidden Evidence: 40 True Crimes and How Forensic Science Helped Solve Them.* Willowdale, ON: Firefly Books, 2000.

*Rainis, Kenneth G. *Blood and DNA Evidence: Crime Solving Experiments.* Berkeley Heights, NJ: Enslow Publishing, 2006.

Ramsland, Katherine. *Beating the Devil's Game: A History of Forensic Science and Criminal Investigation.* New York: Berkeley Books, 2014.

Starr, Douglas P. *The Killer of Little Shepherds: A True Crime Story and the Birth of Forensic Science.* New York: A. A. Knopf, 2010.

*Townsend, John. *Famous Forensic Cases.* Mankato, MN: Amicus, 2012.

*Zullo, Alan. *Crime Scene Investigators.* New York: Scholastic, 2008.

INDEX

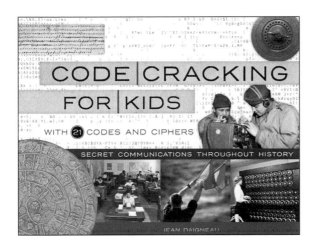

ISBN 978-1-64160-138-2
$18.99 (CAN $24.99)

Code Cracking for Kids

Secret Communications Throughout History, with 21 Codes and Ciphers

By Jean Daigneau

"An engaging, hands-on approach to combine social studies and STEM." —Booklist Online

Throughout history, people have written coded messages to safeguard and pass along secret information and figured out ways to break the coded messages of their enemies and determine what they had planned. The study of these techniques is known as cryptology, and *Code Cracking for Kids* explores many aspects of this fascinating and exciting topic. Kids will read about famous people, such as Julius Caesar and Thomas Jefferson, who invented codes and ciphers; about military codes and codebreaking projects, including Allied efforts to crack Germany's infamous Enigma machine during World War II; and about work being done today by the US government and private-sector experts to safeguard our cybersecurity. Readers will also learn about unsolved ciphers throughout history, codes that can be found in our everyday lives, and devices used by governments and spies to conceal information.

Code Cracking for Kids includes a glossary, a list of online resources, and hands-on activities that allow kids to replicate early code devices and to learn several ciphers to encode and decode their own top-secret messages. Kids will:

* Encrypt a message using a dictionary cipher
* Create a cipher wheel like the one designed by Thomas Jefferson
* Make and write with invisible ink
* Hide a ciphered message inside an egg
* Learn the sounds of Morse code
* And more!

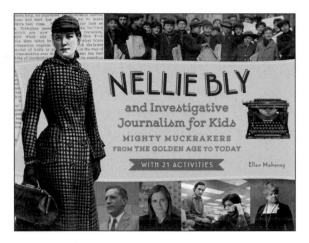

ISBN 978-1-61374-997-5
$16.95 (CAN $19.95)

Nellie Bly and Investigative Journalism for Kids

Mighty Muckrakers from the Golden Age to Today, with 21 Activities

By Ellen Mahoney

"This outstanding work of nonfiction is sure to inspire a new generation of investigative journalists." —*Teacher Librarian*

In the late 1800s, the daring young reporter Elizabeth Cochrane—known by the pen name Nellie Bly—faked insanity so she could be committed to a mental institution and secretly report on the awful conditions there. This and other highly publicized investigative "stunts" laid the groundwork for a new kind of journalism in the early 1900s, called "muckraking," dedicated to exposing social, political, and economic ills in the United States.

In *Nellie Bly and Investigative Journalism for Kids* budding reporters learn about the major figures of the muckraking era: the bold and audacious Bly, one of the most famous women in the world in her day; social reformer and photojournalist Jacob Riis; monopoly buster Ida Tarbell; antilynching crusader Ida B. Wells; and Upton Sinclair, whose classic book *The Jungle* created a public outcry over the dangerous and unsanitary conditions of the early meatpacking industry. Young readers will also learn about more contemporary reporters, from Bob Woodward and Carl Bernstein to Amy Goodman, who have carried on the muckraking tradition, and will get excited about the ever-changing world of journalism and the power of purposeful writing. Twenty-one creative activities encourage and engage a future generation of muckrakers. Kids can:

* Make and keep a reporter's notebook
* Create a Jacob Riis–style photo essay
* Write a letter to the editor
* Craft a "great ideas" box
* And much more